Top 200
Low Fat Recipes

Judith Wills

Photographs by Peter Cassidy

headline

Also by Judith Wills

The Food Bible

Children's Food Bible

The Diet Bible

6 Ways to Lose a Stone in 6 Weeks

The Omega Diet

Slim for Life

The Bodysense Diet

100 Favourite Slim and Healthy Recipes

Slim and Healthy Vegetarian

Copyright © 2003 Judith Wills
Photographs © 2003 Peter Cassidy

The right of Judith Wills to be identified as the Author
of the Work has been asserted by her in accordance with the
Copyright, Designs and Patents Act 1988.

First published in 2003
by HEADLINE BOOK PUBLISHING
First published in paperback in 2005 by Headline Book Publishing

10 9 8 7 6 5 4 3 2 1

Cataloguing in Publication Data is available from the British Library
ISBN 0 7553 1075 6

Set in Helvetica Neau
Designed by Isobel Gillan
Printed and bound in Italy by Canale & C.S.p.A

Headline's policy is to use papers that are natural, renewable and recyclable products
and made from wood grown in sustainable forests. The logging and manufacturing processes
are expected to conform to the environmental regulations of the country of origin.

HEADLINE BOOK PUBLISHING
A division of Hodder Headline
338 Euston Road
London NW1 3BH

www.headline.co.uk
www.hodderheadline.com

SP 00
ecipes

ipes we have come across . . .
veryone's tastebuds'
ss

ents and flavour' *Now*

thout being a martyr to the cause . . .'
nagazine

has excelled herself.
'd dare to try out on friends'
ritionist

. . quick, inviting food
of healthy eating'

and traditional dishes' *Zest*

New Woman

t ideas for every occasion –
ta and Chocolate Mousse look so
y're low fat'
BBC Good Food

contents

introduction

I love planning what to eat. I love cooking. I love eating. And most of all I love the fact that I can do all three without feeling guilty and without spoiling my waistline or damaging my health. The truth is that it isn't difficult to rustle up the most delicious snacks, lunches, salads, suppers, stews and even desserts which are both low in fat and low in calories. This book contains 200 examples to prove the point.

I have spent the past ten years or more testing, adapting and devising recipes which pass my 'taste test' and the other criteria for inclusion in this book – low fat, ease of preparation and, with a few exceptions, reasonable cost. I have also aimed to provide a balance of traditional, much-loved recipes, such as lasagne, coq au vin and pasta carbonara, in a reduced-fat, reduced-calorie format alongside less well-known or new dishes which are naturally light and delicious. On every page there are cooking, ingredient, shopping and preparation tips, and there are plenty of variations on the basic recipes as appropriate.

I don't believe that low-fat cooking means that you have to avoid using small amounts of good quality oils and so you may be surprised to find olive and a few other oils in many recipes, even butter now and then. My cooking is straightforward and easy with no complicated tricks to learn in order to avoid fat.

This chapter contains all you need to know about devising for yourself and your family, a healthy, weight-conscious diet. It also gives meal suggestions for every time of day, including breakfast, and several menu plans to suit all.

I truly believe that the collection of recipes in this book is 'the best' and provides enough variety for anyone who wants to cook in a healthy but enjoyable way for years to come.

Happy cooking!

What makes a healthy low-fat diet?

Healthy eating is most certainly not about cutting all fat out of your diet, nor is it a simple matter of reducing calories. First and foremost, healthy eating is about getting enough of all the nutrients that your body needs for health – a balance of protein, carbohydrate, fibre, vitamins, minerals and even fats that we need for proper functioning. Yes, we all NEED fat.

So why a 'low-fat' cookbook? Simple – the recipes, menu plans and meal suggestions will enable you to reduce fat levels to the internationally agreed acceptable amount of 25 per cent of the total calories in your diet, but, in doing so, they still incorporate enough of the 'healthy fats' that you really do need for good health.

Reduce fat sensibly

These 'healthy fats' are called omega-3 and omega-6, which are part of the polyunsaturated group of fats. In fact, most of us get plenty of omega-6 in our diets and so it is omega-3, which is present in greatest quantity in oily fish and also in some seeds, nuts and vegetables, of which we need to make an effort to eat more. These fats help to keep us healthy in many ways by protecting against heart disease, stroke and some cancers. They are also linked to protection against Alzheimer's disease, arthritis and skin complaints such as eczema, help to protect the immune and reproductive systems and are vital in pregnancy and for a healthy brain.

Another category of healthy fats are the monounsaturated fats, found in greatest quantities in olive oil, rapeseed oil, groundnut oil, avocados and many nuts. These fats are also important in helping to keep a healthy heart, blood cholesterol and blood lipids. I usually use them in cooking as they are more stable than some fats when heated.

The fats that you can cut back on without detriment to your health – and, indeed, reducing them is linked with protection against heart disease and weight problems – are the saturated fats. These fats are found in greatest quantities in full-fat dairy produce, such as full-cream milk, cream, hard and cream cheeses and butter, and also in fatty cuts of meat, such as shoulder of lamb, stewing beef, pork crackling, as well as in lard and in many commercially made products, including pastries, pies, cakes, biscuits, desserts and much more. These commercial products are also likely to contain undesirable levels of trans or hydrogenated fats – commercially hardened polyunsaturated fats.

Saturated fats and trans fats are those closely linked with the increased risk of heart disease, stroke and other circulatory diseases and, because they are often present in foods that are also high in sugar and/or calories, with obesity. Cut back on these foods and you can save hundreds of calories and many grams of fat a day without hunger and without pain.

Fat, slimming and weight control

Many of us want to cut back on fat because we believe it is an easy way to cut calories, as well as a healthier way to eat. Indeed, research shows that cutting down on the amount of fat that you eat is the simplest way to lose weight and the easiest way to stay slim long term.

The United States Department of Agriculture (USDA) states that people who cut fat – even while making no other changes to their diets – lose weight steadily, and that it is people who maintain a reduced-fat diet (and take regular exercise) who manage to keep the weight off.

The best type of low-fat diet to follow, the USDA and the World Health Organisation recommend, is not, however, an extremely low-fat diet (one that contains around 10–15 per cent of your daily calories as fat) but a moderately low-fat diet that contains around 25 per cent fat.

introduction

The 25 per cent level – achieved by cutting intake of saturated and trans fats, while retaining omega-3 and -6 in the diet – seems to be the one which provides a range of health benefits, while offering the most chance of success in weight control. This is partly because it is not unworkably low in fat. Very low-fat diets have what is termed 'low compliance', since people don't stick to them for long because they find them boring, restrictive and unpalatable. By the way, fat occurs naturally in a wide range of healthy foods (almost all foods, even green vegetables and grains, for instance) so the concept of a 'fat-free' diet is actually impossible unless you fast – another bad idea!

The recipes in this book, when eaten as part of a balanced meal with the suggested accompaniments as appropriate, will help you to keep to a 25 per cent fat diet, and restrict saturated fats but not the other healthier fats.

The chart below shows you how much fat you should aim to eat a day, both for weight control and for slimming, including my guidelines on how much of that fat you might eat at each meal. Remember it's all about balance – if you choose a higher-fat main meal, then pick a lower-fat lunch.

Keep it low every day

Obviously, the recipes in this book are all low in fat but when preparing breakfasts, snacks and other non-recipe lunches and main meals, you can easily keep fat down to healthy levels by using the following tips:

- Right now, go through your larder, chuck out old/stale/boring/high-fat items. Make a list and restock with plenty of low-fat, low-cal seasonings, canned tomatoes, pulses, pasta, wholegrains and other items using ideas from the checklist opposite.
- Invest in a few good quality cooking utensils (see ideas opposite) which will help you to reduce the amount of fat needed in cooking.
- Cheese lovers will be relieved to hear that a small amount of very strong cheese, such as real Parmesan, extra-mature farmhouse Cheddar or Gruyère, goes a long way in cooking and may in the end save you more fat and calories than a portion of a reduced-fat, mild cheese, while also being better for your psyche. Grating cheese also makes it go further.

The amount of fat you need a day

	Typical adult female*	
	slimming diet (1,500 calories a day) 25% fat	weight maintenance diet (2,000 calories a day) 25% fat
Total grams of fat needed	42g	56g
Sample breakdown**		
Breakfast	5g	5–8g
Lunch	12–15g	15–18g
Evening meal	17–20g	20–25g
Snacks/desserts	5g	5–10g

*Males should increase weight maintenance and slimming calories and fat by 25 per cent.

**For guidance only; the exact amount of fat that you eat at each meal isn't important as long as your overall daily fat intake is within the guidelines.

- Always use a cooking oil spray (available in ready-to-use spray pump cans at the supermarket, or you can buy your own empty spray can and fill it according to the manufacturer's instructions) instead of pouring oil into the pan when frying and browning foods such as meat, bacon and poultry.
- Always buy the leaner cuts of meat, often labelled 'extra lean' or 'less than 10 per cent' or '5 per cent' fat. Some pundits will tell you that these lean cuts don't give enough flavour or moisture to a finished dish, or may be tough, but if you cook them correctly this needn't be the case, and I certainly don't find them so.
- Make full use of the naturally low-fat cooking methods, such as grilling, griddling, steaming, poaching, baking and cooking in parchment.
- Make full use of naturally low-fat meals, such as vegetable soups, white fish, pulses, pasta and other grains with vegetable sauces, salads with a simple low-fat dressing, sandwiches with low-fat fillings, such as turkey, lean ham, skinless chicken and plenty of salad.
- Include plenty of naturally tasty seasonings in your meals – fresh herbs, fresh and dried spices, vinegars, soy and Worcestershire sauce, citrus juices, mushroom ketchup, sun-dried vacuum-packed tomatoes, and so on. These will help to satisfy tastebuds, which are used to getting flavour from fat.
- Eat smaller portions of the higher-fat foods such as meat, moderate-fat cheese, full-fat yogurt and desserts, and larger portions of vegetables, salad, fruit and very low-fat protein foods like skimmed milk, low-fat yogurt and low-fat fromage frais. If your plate is full and looks attractive with plenty of colours and textures, you will not feel as if you are being deprived. But don't feel you have to give up these higher-fat foods completely – many of them offer a good range of nutrients, including calcium and protein in cheese, and iron and protein in red meat.
- For sandwiches and things on toast you can do without butter or other high-fat spreads. To prevent salad-filled sandwiches from going soggy, spread the bread very lightly with reduced-calorie mayonnaise (such as Hellmann's Light), which also adds taste and moisture.
- Aim for plenty of variety in your diet – boredom is a killer for a food lover, and can make you think you are hungry/crave a box of chocolates.
- Shop wisely, when you aren't hungry. What you don't buy, you can't eat.

Vegetarian recipes

Vegetarian recipes are indicated with a ⓥ symbol.

Kitchen utensils

You may already have all the utensils you need for low-fat cooking – check down this list to see what I consider almost essential (over and above the things you are bound to have, such as a few saucepans, stirring spoons and so on).

- A really good quality, heavy non-stick frying pan or even better, one large one and one small one.
- A casserole dish with a tight-fitting lid, preferably a flameproof one, which will save you a lot of bother when cooking stews, braises and casseroles.
- A really good quality, heavy baking tray for roasting vegetables, etc. A cheap thin one will tend to burn not bake your food.
- A couple of heatproof, non-metal curved spatulas for sautéing and a couple of flat, heatproof, non-metal spatulas for turning food in your non-stick pan.

You might also like to consider a ridged cast iron griddle pan, a lifetime investment for the committed griller, and decent kitchen scales, which weigh in small increments of 2g. A lot of cheaper kitchen scales don't weigh less than 20g accurately, which is important for both calories and fats (if you are weighing out butter or cheese, for example) and for precision cooking, such as most baking and desserts.

Planning your low-fat diet

Whether you want to lose weight or simply cut down on the amount of fat you eat, the following suggestions will help you devise a diet that suits. Try to mix and match your meals so that you eat a wide variety of food types – if you have meat in the evening, have a vegetarian or fish lunch, for example. Drink plenty of water – aim for six glasses a day – and don't go overboard on high-caffeine drinks. Remember there are calories in most drinks; allow yourself a 200–250ml skimmed milk allowance a day for use in hot drinks or on its own.

For slimming

Select one of the following suggestions or the recipes in this book to give a maximum total fat intake of 42g a day. Try to ensure that your daily calorie total adds up to no more than 1,500 (for women) but no less than 1,250 (eat extra low-fat snacks if your chosen meals don't add up to at least this). Men can increase calorie and fat intake by 25 per cent for weight loss. Each day:

● choose from one of the following breakfasts (5g fat maximum)
● choose from one of the following snacks or a dessert (5g fat maximum)
● select a recipe lunch – a soup, snack or salad, for example (12–15g fat)
● select a recipe main meal – a quick hob supper, pasta, grill or stew, for example (17–20g fat).

Breakfasts *(maximum 250 calories; 5g fat)*

● 125ml pot low-fat natural bio yogurt with 25g muesli, 1 teaspoon linseeds and 1 chopped apple.
● 100g pot low-fat fruit diet fromage frais; 25g slice wholemeal bread with 1 teaspoon low-fat spread and 2 teaspoons low-sugar marmalade; 1 small banana.
● 5 tablespoons baked beans on 40g slice wholemeal bread; 1 glass orange juice.
● 2 Weetabix or 30g unsweetened breakfast cereal (not muesli) with 125ml skimmed milk; 25g slice wholemeal bread with 1 teaspoon low-fat spread and 1 teaspoon Marmite.

Snacks *(maximum 100 calories; 5g fat)*

● 100g pot low-fat fruit diet fromage frais; 1 satsuma, plum or kiwifruit.
● 2 dark rye crispbread topped with 1 tablespoon low-fat soft cheese, cherry tomatoes or apple slices.
● 25g slice wholemeal bread with 1 teaspoon low-fat spread and Marmite.
● 1 medium banana and 3 ready-to-eat dried apricots.

For weight maintenance

Select one of the following suggestions or the recipes in this book to give a maximum total fat intake of 56g a day. Try to ensure that your daily calorie total adds up to no more than 2,000 (for women), so if your chosen meals come to less than this eat extra low-fat snacks. Men can increase calorie and fat intake by 25 per cent. Each day:

● choose from one of the following breakfasts (maximum 8g fat)
● choose from one of the following snacks (maximum 10g fat)

- select a recipe lunch (15–18g fat)
- select a recipe main meal (20–25g fat).

Breakfasts *(maximum 350 calories; 8g fat)*

- 60g luxury muesli with 125ml skimmed milk, topped with 1 chopped apple and 1 segmented tangerine.
- 40g Fruit 'n Fibre with 125ml skimmed milk, topped with 100g berry fruits or 1 kiwifruit; 40g slice wholemeal bread with 1 teaspoon low-fat spread and 2 teaspoons low-sugar jam.
- 1 medium egg, boiled, with 40g slice wholemeal bread with 1 teaspoon low-fat spread; 1 medium banana; 100ml glass orange juice.
- 3 medium tomatoes, halved and fried in a non-stick pan with 1 teaspoon butter on 40g slice wholemeal toast; 125ml pot low-fat diet fruit yogurt.

Snacks *(maximum 200 calories; 10g fat)*

- 1 large plain digestive biscuit; 1 dessertspoon pumpkin seeds; 1 apple.
- Sandwich made with 2 × 25g slices wholemeal bread, filled with sliced tomato and 2 slices extra-lean ham; 1 orange.
- 150g pot low-fat rice pudding; 1 apple or pear.
- 300ml any New Covent Garden vegetable soup; 2 dark rye Ryvitas.
- Sandwich made with 2 × 25g slices brown bread, spread with low-fat mayonnaise and filled with 50g tuna in water or brine, well drained, and lettuce.
- 1 slice Sultana Malt Loaf (see page 213) with 1 teaspoon low-fat spread.
- 1 oblong piece Apricot and Apple Flapjacks (see page 212); 1 kiwifruit or plum.

Dinner party menus

If you're planning a supper party for friends or family, balance your menu so that there is a complementary mix of flavours, ingredients and styles. Remember the following tips:

- Meals often work best when each course comes from a similar area of the world.
- If you're having meat for your main course, avoid a meat starter. The same applies to fish, chicken, cheese and pulses.
- If you have a soup starter, go for a 'dry' main course, while a 'dry' starter can be happily followed by a gravy-rich main course or casserole.
- You need have no more than one, or at most two, hot courses. In summer, they can all be cold.
- Don't have the same dominant flavour in more than one course – tomato sauce, for instance, or a strong herb such as basil or coriander.
- If one of your courses is relatively high in fat, pick a low-fat starter and dessert.
- Aim for no more than 30g fat per portion for a special occasion three-course meal, a figure which should fit in reasonably well with most people's low-fat diets – although it is possible to devise many three-course meals from the recipes in this book for much less than that.

introduction

menu one **summer**

Chilled Cucumber Soup (see page 38)

Salmon and Avocado Salad (see page 193)

Wholemeal rolls

Summer Berry Pavlova (see page 198)

Total fat: 29g

menu two **summer**

Mixed Pepper Bruschetta (see page 26)

Fettucine with Broad Beans and Prosciutto
(see page 158)

Green salad

Strawberry and Nut Gâteau (see page 206)

Total fat: 27.5g

menu three **autumn**

Moules Marinière (see page 23)

Steak au Poivre (see page 122)

Mangetout and new potatoes, each portion
garnished with 1 teaspoon butter

Pears in Rosé Wine (see page 204)

Total fat: 23g

menu four **autumn**

Marinated Garlic Mushrooms (see page 28)

Crusty white bread

Pesto-stuffed Chicken Breasts (see page 106)

Ginger Plum Custard (see page 200)

Total fat: 22g

menu five **winter**

Chickpea Soup with Lemon (see page 38)

Lamb and Orzo Gratin (see page 155)

Broccoli and peas

Sparkling Wine and Grape Jellies (see page 197)

Total fat: 24g

menu six **winter**

Chicken Noodle Soup (see page 41)

Sushi Selection (see page 164)

Fresh exotic fruits

Total fat: 11g

menu seven **spring**

Vichyssoise (see page 48)

Beef Bourguignon (see page 70)

New potatoes and green beans

Pancakes with Pineapple and Banana
(see page 205)

Total fat: 21g

menu eight **spring**

Half portions of Pasta with Garlic Mushrooms
(see page 173)

Tuna Catalan (see page 141)

Rice and green salad

Chocolate Mousses with Raspberry Coulis
(see page 209)

Total fat: 30.5g

menu nine **vegetarian**

Wild Mushroom Soup (see page 35)

Winter Root Vegetable Bake (see page 118)

Raspberry and Marsala Trifle (see page 196)

Total fat: 29g

menu ten **vegetarian**

Guacamole Toasts (see page 31)

Pasta Primavera (see page 171)

Summer Fruit Kebabs (see page 201)

Total fat: 27.5g

menu eleven **quick and easy**

Seared Scallops with Roast Cherry Tomatoes
(see page 22)

Steak with Garlic and Red Wine (see page 126)

New potatoes and peas

Summer Fruit Kebabs (see page 201)

Total fat: 23g

menu twelve **quick and easy**

Smoked Trout Pâté (see page 16)

Mustard Pork Kebabs (see page 56)

Rice and green salad

Strawberry Brûlée (see page 200)

Total fat: 23g

introduction

snacks and starters

The recipes in this chapter can also be served as a light lunch or supper, or as a starter for a dinner party. Many of the soup recipes in the next chapter, the salad recipes on pages 176–94 and half portions of some of the pasta and grain recipes on pages 150–75 are also suitable as snacks or starters.

When choosing a starter for a three-course meal, aim to restrict the fat content to no more than 8g per portion – or another way to provide a healthy balanced meal is to aim for a maximum of 30g fat for the whole meal and pick your three courses from the various chapters in this book accordingly.

There are many other quick and easy ideas for snacks and starters that don't really need a recipe. Try griddled thinly sliced Mediterranean vegetables, such as aubergines or courgettes, drizzled with a little olive oil and balsamic vinegar, for example, or roasted asparagus or baby vine tomatoes with a vinaigrette or a squeeze of lemon juice and black pepper.

Fruits, of course, are an ideal low-fat and low-calorie starter. You need not feel guilty about serving a simple ripe, juicy, orange-fleshed melon or plump fresh figs, or try sprinkling red grapefruit segments with sugar, grill them and serve with a green salad.

You could serve a selection of vegetable crudités, such as carrot, celery, onion and chicory, with a simple tzatziki-type dip of Greek yogurt, garlic and cucumber with seasoning. For a spicy dip, mix the yogurt with a little tomato sauce and finely chopped chilli.

If your main meal is one of the heartier, higher-calorie selections in this book, no one will want a substantial starter, so don't be afraid to serve just a well-dressed green salad.

gravadlax with dill and mustard sauce

Salmon is a high-fat fish, but the oils are mainly the 'good for you' omega-3 type that you should still eat regularly even if cutting back on your fat intake. Gravadlax is a Scandinavian cured salmon dish, and makes a great change from smoked salmon. It is usually served with a very high-fat dill and mustard sauce made with eggs, oil and double cream – my version is much lighter but just as nice.

Serves 4 | 215 calories per portion | 11.5g fat per portion

good bunch or pot of fresh dill, finely chopped

2 tbsp sea salt

2 tbsp sugar

1 tbsp crushed black peppercorns

2 plump, top quality fresh salmon fillets (about 150g each), skin on

FOR THE SAUCE

75ml half-fat crème fraîche

1 tbsp Dijon mustard

1 tbsp lemon juice

1 heaped tsp caster sugar

salt and black pepper

1 To make the gravadlax, mix two-thirds of the dill with the salt, sugar and peppercorns. Spoon a quarter of the mixture into a non-metallic dish that will accommodate the fillets of salmon placed on top of each other. Put a salmon fillet on top (skin-side down) and spread half of the dill mixture over it, then place the second salmon fillet (skin-side up) on top of the first and rub the remaining dill mixture over the fish.

2 Cover the salmon with clingfilm and weigh it down using a saucer or similar with a heavy can on top, for example. It's vital that you do compress the fish in this way. Leave the salmon in the fridge for at least two days, turning it once or twice – the marinading mixture will cure the fish.

3 An hour or two before you want to eat, make the sauce. In a bowl, combine the crème fraîche with the mustard, then stir in the remaining chopped dill. Mix together the lemon juice and sugar, until the sugar begins to dissolve, and stir it into the sauce, then season to taste.

4 To serve the fish, pat it dry (leaving some of the dill and pepper on the surfaces) and thinly slice it diagonally towards the thinner end of the fillet, discarding the skin. Serve each portion with a spoonful of the sauce.

serving suggestion You can serve the gravadlax with thin slices of brown bread, spread with low-fat spread, or try ready-made blinis.

melon, prosciutto and ginger salad

Serves 4 | 60 calories per portion | 3g fat per portion

70g pack prosciutto
(Parma ham)

cooking oil spray (optional)

1 ripe Cantaloupe melon, sliced into
wedges and peeled, reserving
any juice

1 dsp balsamic vinegar

1.5cm piece of fresh root ginger,
very finely grated

fresh mint leaves, to garnish

1 Preheat the grill to medium. Grill the prosciutto, or spray a non-stick frying pan with a little cooking oil and fry until crisp. Allow to cool a little, then roughly crumble and set aside.

2 Arrange the melon slices on four serving plates and scatter the prosciutto on top.

3 Combine any juices from the melon with the balsamic vinegar and the ginger, mixing well (see Tip). Drizzle the dressing over the melon and garnish with mint leaves.

tip If your melon doesn't yield much juice, add 1 tablespoon of orange or apple juice to the vinegar and ginger mixture.

snacks and starters

smoked trout pâté

Serves 4 | 100 calories per portion | 6g fat per portion

175g smoked trout fillets
(weight without skin; see Tips)

1 dsp creamy horseradish sauce

75g fromage frais, 8% fat

30ml light mayonnaise

juice of ½ lemon

sweet paprika

black pepper

rocket or watercress and lemon
wedges, to garnish

brown toast, to serve

1 Flake the trout into a mixing bowl, add the remaining ingredients, up to and excluding the garnishes and blend together until you have a rough pâté.

2 Divide the mixture between four ramekin dishes and smooth down. Sprinkle sweet paprika evenly on top. Chill for 1 hour or until required.

3 Serve the pâté in the ramekins on plates, garnished with the rocket or watercress and lemon wedges, with some brown toast.

serving suggestion This pâté makes an ideal sandwich filling.

Don't buy the flat packs of sliced smoked trout that's a ringer for smoked salmon – the trout you want for this recipe is the whole plump fillets, which are usually sold in supermarkets next to the smoked mackerel. Smoked mackerel makes a similarly good pâté.

grilled prawn skewers with thai dip

Serves 4 | 100 calories per portion | 3g fat per portion

16 large raw king prawns (about 25g each), heads removed, tails left on
1 large clove garlic, crushed
1 fresh red chilli, deseeded and finely chopped
1 dsp sesame oil
2 tbsp soy sauce
grated zest of 1 lime
1 tbsp chopped fresh coriander, to garnish

FOR THE DIP
2 tbsp soy sauce
1 tbsp Thai fish sauce (nam pla)
25g soft dark brown sugar
juice of 1 lime
1 tsp chilli sauce

1 Arrange the prawns in a single layer in a glass dish. Mix together the remaining marinade ingredients, except the coriander, and pour the mixture over the prawns; leave, covered, in the fridge for 1–2 hours.

2 To make the dip, mix together all the ingredients in a small saucepan and bring to the boil, stirring. Take off the heat, leave to cool and pour into a serving bowl.

3 Just before you are ready to eat, thread the prawns on to four small kebab sticks. Preheat the grill (or a ridged griddle pan) to high and cook the prawns for a few minutes, turning once and brushing again with the marinade, until pink and cooked through.

4 Serve the prawns with the dipping sauce, garnished with the coriander.

17

snacks and starters

antipasto

This classic Italian starter salad usually comprises a selection of appetising vegetables and meats, similar to the Spanish tapas or Greek meze, and is often laid out on a large platter. My version cuts the fat but not the taste or visual appeal and can be served as either a starter or light lunch.

Serves 4 | 200 calories per portion | 13.5g fat per portion

1 tbsp olive oil

1 dsp lemon juice

2 medium courgettes, thinly sliced lengthways (see Tip)

4 canned artichoke hearts, well drained

125g ball Italian mozzarella, well drained, and torn into rough pieces

8 cherry tomatoes, halved

4 slices prosciutto (Parma ham – see Tip)

4 slices bresaola

2 fresh ripe figs, halved (optional – see Tip)

8 black stoned olives

few fresh basil leaves, to garnish

1 Mix together the oil and lemon juice, and pour this marinade over the courgettes in a bowl, stirring to combine well. If you have time, leave to marinate for 1–2 hours.

2 Preheat the grill to very hot. Place the courgettes directly on the rack, reserving the marinade, and grill for 2–3 minutes each side until softened and patterned with the rack marks. Alternatively, you can use a ridged griddle pan.

3 Fold the courgettes and arrange in two areas of a large serving platter.

4 Arrange the artichokes and mozzarella with the tomatoes, meats and figs on the platter so that they look attractive.

5 Scatter the olives over the platter and drizzle the remaining oil and lemon marinade over the tomatoes, mozzarella and artichokes. Garnish with the basil leaves and serve.

serving suggestions You could divide everything up equally into four and serve it on individual platters instead, if preferred.

Crusty Italian bread makes a good accompaniment for a light lunch.

If using as a starter, a meat-free pasta dish would make a suitable main course.

tips You can use asparagus or aubergine slices instead of the courgettes, cooked in the same way.

Prosciutto is very thinly sliced air-dried Italian ham. You could substitute other similar hams, such as those from Germany or even four rashers of very thinly sliced, extra lean bacon, in which case the calories and fat count will be a little higher.

If you don't want to use the figs, or they are out of season, you could simply omit them (12 calories less per portion) or substitute some slices of fresh ripe mango (not authentic, but still nice!) or melon.

seafood cocktails

Old-fashioned and simple, seafood cocktails are nevertheless hard to resist.
The tang of the sun-dried tomatoes gives this seafood sauce a fantastic taste and
no one will be able to tell that it is low in fat.

Serves 4 | 155 calories per portion | 7.5g fat per portion

50g cos, romaine or iceberg
lettuce, leaves torn
350g top quality seafood of choice,
such as peeled prawns, shrimps,
mussels, crab, or a mixture,
clean and dried (see Tip)
1 tsp sweet paprika
4 lemon wedges, to garnish

FOR THE SAUCE
2 tbsp ready-made mayonnaise
(full-fat type)
3 tbsp low-fat natural bio yogurt
1 dsp good quality sun-dried
tomato paste from a jar
1 dsp lemon juice
1 dash of Tabasco
1 dash of Worcestershire sauce
1 tsp Dijon mustard
pinch of caster sugar
salt and black pepper

1 To make the sauce, mix together all the ingredients in a bowl until well combined. Taste and adjust the seasoning as necessary.

2 Divide the lettuce between four glass serving dishes.

3 Spoon the seafood on top of the leaves and pour the dressing over.

4 Sprinkle the paprika over and garnish with lemon wedges (see Tip).

tips The cocktail isn't as nice if you use poor quality seafood; try to avoid frozen bulk-buy prawns or frozen packs of mixed seafood.
Garnish with whole shell-on prawns, if you like.

crab salad with avocado dressing

Crab is low in fat and calories, while avocado and olive oil are high in fat of the healthy monounsaturated kind and packed with the antioxidant vitamin E, which isn't that easy to come by in a low-fat diet. Combine the two and you get the best of both worlds as well as a gorgeous combination of flavours.

Serves 4 | 180 calories per portion | 14g fat per portion

8 asparagus tips (optional – see Tip)

1 large fully ripe avocado, halved and stoned

1 tbsp olive oil

1 tbsp light mayonnaise (see Tip)

2 tbsp low-fat natural bio yogurt

1 tbsp lemon juice

salt and black pepper

2 tbsp skimmed milk

200g fresh or frozen white crab meat

12 rosettes of lamb's lettuce or watercress sprigs, to garnish

1 Cook the asparagus tips until just softened, drain and refresh under cold water; set aside (see Tip).

2 Using a fairly flat tablespoon or serving spoon, carefully remove most of the avocado flesh from each half, in a complete piece if possible, leaving behind some of the deep green flesh right next to the skin.

3 Slice the avocado crossways and arrange the slices on four serving plates, then spoon the deep green flesh from the skins and put it into a small mixing bowl (you only need a dessertspoon or so of this so don't worry if there isn't a lot).

4 Add the oil, mayonnaise, yogurt and lemon juice to the bowl with a good twist of seasoning and beat together with a fork or, if you have one, a mini electric blender, which will produce a smoother consistency. Add half the skimmed milk (you may not need all of it) to the bowl and blend again. The sauce should have the same consistency as pouring custard; if not, add the rest of the milk and blend once more. Check the seasoning.

5 Arrange the crab meat over the avocado slices, then drizzle the avocado sauce over and top with the asparagus tips. Place the lamb's lettuce or watercress around the edge of the plates and serve.

serving suggestion Serve the salad with brown or walnut bread.

tips Garnish the top of the salad with a rosette of lamb's lettuce or watercress instead, if you prefer.

Light mayonnaise (several brands available) may also be called 'half-fat' mayonnaise.

Prepare the rest of the salad just before serving as the avocado flesh discolours if it is exposed to the air for more than a few minutes.

snacks and starters

seared scallops with roast cherry tomatoes

Scallops are very low in fat and lower in cholesterol than other shellfish, while tomatoes are rich in antioxidants, such as vitamins C and E and the plant chemical, lycopene. Feel virtuous while you enjoy!

Serves 4 | 95 calories per portion | 5.5g fat per portion

1 pack cherry tomatoes (about 250g)
2 cloves garlic, chopped
2 bay leaves, crushed
1 dsp chopped fresh thyme
1 tsp chopped fresh rosemary
salt and black pepper
1½ tbsp olive oil
cooking oil spray (optional)
8 large, good quality king scallops or 12 smaller (about 200g)
squeeze of lemon juice
rocket leaves, to garnish

1 Arrange the tomatoes in a suitably sized baking tray. Sprinkle with the garlic, herbs and seasoning and drizzle over most of the olive oil. Roast in a preheated oven, 200°C/400°F/Gas 6, for about 30 minutes or until the tomatoes have softened but still retain their shape, and there are plenty of nice juices in the pan.

2 When the tomatoes are nearly ready, preheat a griddle pan (or a good quality, non-stick frying pan coated with cooking oil spray) until very hot. Meanwhile, make sure the scallops are dry and brush the flat sides with the remaining olive oil.

3 Add the scallops to the pan and, without moving them, sear for about 1½ minutes, a little more or less depending on size (see Tip). Turn them over and sear the other side.

4 Just before the scallops are ready, spoon the tomatoes on to serving plates using a slotted spatula. Place the scallops on the plates, then add a squeeze of lemon to the 'tomatoey' pan juices and drizzle them over the top. Serve immediately, garnished with rocket leaves.

tip Do make sure the pan is very hot before adding the scallops and don't try to move them until they have had time to seal in the pan or they will stick.

moules marinière

Mussels are very low in calories and high on taste so are ideal for weight watchers. The small amount of butter added to this recipe is well justified. Much better to have a little top quality butter now and then than tasteless half-fat spreads every day!

Serves 4 | 170 calories per portion | 8g fat per portion

20g butter
4 shallots, very finely chopped
2 cloves garlic, finely chopped
200ml dry white wine
100ml fish stock (see Tip)
1 tbsp chopped fresh parsley
1kg mussels in their shells, cleaned (see Tip)
40ml single cream (see Tip)
squeeze of lemon juice
pepper

1 Heat the butter in a large non-stick flameproof casserole with a tight-fitting lid. Sweat the shallots over a medium-high heat for 10–15 minutes or until softened but not browned.

2 Add the garlic, wine, fish stock and half the parsley and bring to the boil. Tip the prepared mussels into the pan, cover and reduce the heat to medium.

3 Look at the mussels after 5 minutes, by which time they should have opened (see Tip). Discard any that remain closed and transfer the others with a slotted spoon to a large bowl and keep warm (cover with foil or place at the back of the hob or in a low oven).

4 Bring the cooking liquor back to the boil and cook fast for a few minutes until reduced a little. Add the cream and a squeeze of lemon juice, and season with pepper (you shouldn't need salt).

5 Divide the mussels between serving dishes and pour the sauce over, then sprinkle with the remaining parsley to garnish.

serving suggestion Serve the mussels with crusty bread to soak up the delicious juices.

tips Try to find ready-made fresh fish stock at the supermarket – it's much nicer than fish stock made with a cube.

You can buy mussels ready-cleaned, but if not, put them in a large sieve and rinse under cold running water, pulling off any beards. Throw away any with cracked shells, and those that remain open when tapped. After cooking, it's important to discard any that haven't opened.

Instead of using cream, you could stir 100g chopped canned tomatoes into the sauce to reduce the fat content even further (20 calories and 2g fat less per portion).

Don't overcook the mussels or they may turn rubbery.

snacks and starters

ⓥ creamy cheese dip with crudités

This tasty dip contains a quarter of the calories of one made with cream cheese. Yes, it contains high-fat blue cheese, but it is so tangy that a very little goes a long way.

Serves 3–4 as a starter | For 4: 70 calories per portion | 4g fat per portion
For 3: 95 calories per portion | 5.5g fat per portion

1 tbsp light mayonnaise
20ml ricotta cheese
20ml fromage frais, 0% fat
1 tbsp low-fat soft cheese
25g Dolcelatte cheese (see Tip)
20ml skimmed milk
1 tsp Dijon mustard
squeeze of lemon juice
1 dsp chopped fresh chives
salt and black pepper

FOR THE CRUDITÉS
2 sticks celery, cut into 5cm lengths
2 hearts of little gem lettuce, leaves separated
5cm piece of cucumber, deseeded and cut into sticks
4 spring onions, cut into 5cm lengths
1 medium carrot, cut into 5cm lengths
2 grissini sticks, halved

1 In a mixing bowl, beat together the first five ingredients thoroughly, then add the skimmed milk and mix again.

2 Stir in the mustard, lemon juice and chives and season to taste. If the mixture seems too thick, thin with a little extra skimmed milk to a good dipping consistency.

3 Serve the dip in ramekins with the vegetable crudités and the grissini sticks.

serving suggestion This is good as part of a party buffet and also makes a nice topping for a baked potato or a low-fat cheese sandwich filling with salad.

tip If you can't find Dolcelatte cheese, use St Agur, Roquefort or any tangy soft blue cheese, although Stilton is a bit too hard to mix well.
The dip will keep for a day or two, covered, in the fridge.

ⓥ cannellini bean and lemon spread pitta pockets

This is a nice variation on traditional hummus – the cannellini beans are milder than chickpeas and have a creamier texture.

Serves 4 as a hearty starter or snack | 325 calories per portion | 14.5g fat per portion

3 tbsp olive oil
2 shallots, finely chopped
2 cloves garlic, finely chopped
400g can cannellini beans in water, drained, reserving the liquid (see Tip)
grated zest and juice of 1 lemon
dash of Tabasco
1–2 tbsp low-fat natural bio yogurt (optional)
salt and black pepper
1 dsp balsamic vinegar

TO SERVE
tomato, crisp lettuce and cucumber, chopped
4 wholewheat pitta breads, split lengthways

1 Heat a third of the oil in a non-stick frying pan and sauté the shallots for 10 minutes until softened, then add the garlic and fry for another 1–2 minutes. Set the pan aside.

2 Add the beans with the contents of the frying pan to a mixing bowl with 25ml of the reserved water, the second third of the oil, the lemon zest and juice and the Tabasco, and mash thoroughly (see Tips). If the mixture is too stiff, add extra water or yogurt. Season to taste.

3 Serve the pâté with the tomato, lettuce and cucumber divided between the pitta bread pockets. Mix the remaining oil with the balsamic vinegar and drizzle it over the pitta pockets.

tips You can make a low-fat hummus using this recipe but substitute canned chickpeas for the cannellini beans.

Read the label to make sure the beans aren't canned in brine, since the liquid will be far too salty to use in this recipe.

You could purée the bean mixture in an electric blender or food processor, but be careful not to overblend.

ⓥ mixed pepper bruschetta

This is an ideal Italian starter to serve before roast cod, or lamb stew with lemon and tomato, for example.

Serves 4 | 190 calories per portion | 5g fat per portion

2 medium red peppers (about 100g each), halved and deseeded
2 medium yellow peppers (about 100g each), halved and deseeded
2 cloves garlic, peeled
1 tbsp olive oil
1 tsp balsamic vinegar
salt and black pepper
8 × 1cm thick slices ciabatta bread (about 200g total weight)
fresh basil and mint, to garnish

1 Preheat the grill to high and grill the peppers for 15 minutes or until slightly charred and softened. Transfer to a bowl, cover and set aside to cool.

2 When cool, peel off the skins (over the bowl, as the tasty juices will escape while you are doing this) and cut the peppers into strips lengthways.

3 Return the peppers to the bowl. Crush one of the garlic cloves and add this to the bowl with half the oil, the vinegar and seasoning. Stir very well and then tip the pepper mixture into a small non-stick pan and keep warm over a medium-low heat while you toast the bread.

4 Toast or bake the slices of bread until golden, rub with the remaining whole garlic clove and drizzle with the rest of the oil. Put the toasts on serving plates and top with the pepper mixture, including all the juices (see Tip). Garnish with fresh basil and mint, and serve immediately.

serving suggestion Basic bruschetta (bread, baked or toasted, rubbed with garlic and drizzled with oil) is very good with soup or a salad.

tip For a more substantial snack or to add protein, crumble 25g feta cheese or break up 25g Italian mozzarella or grate 15g Parmesan per person over the top of the peppers. This will add about 70 calories and 5g fat per portion.

ⓥ marinated garlic mushrooms

This is a quick and easy starter for when you have friends round, but try to leave the mushrooms to marinate in the liquor for several hours.

Serves 4 | 70 calories per portion | 5.5g fat per portion

20ml olive oil

3 large cloves garlic, very finely chopped

1 tsp ground coriander seeds

250g small mushrooms or mixed wild mushrooms (see Tip)

2 tbsp lemon juice

100ml passata

1 tsp soft dark brown sugar

salt and black pepper

chopped fresh coriander, to garnish

1 Heat the oil in a non-stick frying pan and sweat the garlic over a medium heat for a few minutes; add the ground coriander and stir for a minute more. Add the mushrooms and stir to coat.

2 Add the remaining ingredients, except the fresh coriander, and bring to a simmer, then take off the heat and leave to cool.

3 Pour into a lidded, non-metallic container and refrigerate for a few hours or overnight. If the marinade doesn't completely cover the mushrooms, stir occasionally.

4 To serve, heat the contents of the container (if it is microwaveable, you can do this on medium microwave power for about 3 minutes). Divide the mushrooms between small serving dishes and garnish with chopped fresh coriander.

serving suggestions The mushrooms are also good served cold. Crusty bread makes the best accompaniment, to mop up the garlicky sauce.

tip Try to find the tastiest mushrooms that you can – often the very small supermarket button mushrooms lack flavour. In fact, large sliced mushrooms will taste just as good here but won't look quite so pretty in the dish!

gratin of portobello mushrooms

Portobello or field mushrooms make a great base for a delicious savoury filling, which includes Gruyère cheese. This strong, nutty, flavoursome cheese is ideal for fat-watchers as a little goes a very long way. The gratin makes an ideal dinner party starter.

Serves 4 | 120 calories per portion | 6g fat per portion

4 rashers extra-lean smoked back bacon, finely chopped (see Tip)

½ tbsp olive oil

2–3 spring onions, finely chopped

2 cloves garlic, finely chopped

4 large portobello or dark-gilled field mushrooms, stalks finely chopped (see Tip)

2–3 tbsp vegetable stock

1 tbsp lemon juice

40g white breadcrumbs

25g Gruyère cheese, grated

1 tbsp chopped fresh parsley

salt and black pepper

cooking oil spray (see Tip)

few frisée leaves, to garnish

balsamic vinegar, to serve

1 Put the bacon into a small non-stick frying pan and gradually heat the pan so that the bacon cooks in its own fat. Increase the heat and crisp the bacon pieces towards the end of cooking.

2 Reduce the heat and add the oil, spring onions and garlic to the pan. Stir-fry for 1–2 minutes until softened, then add mushrooms stalks and 1 tablespoon of the vegetable stock to the mixture. Stir until the stalks have softened, then add the lemon juice.

3 In a bowl, mix together the breadcrumbs, most of the cheese, parsley and seasoning, then add the contents of the frying pan, stirring well to combine.

4 Put the mushrooms on a baking tray and drizzle the rest of the vegetable stock over the gills and divide the stuffing mixture neatly between the mushrooms. Top with the remaining cheese and spray each of them with a few squirts of the cooking oil.

5 Cook in a preheated oven, 200°C/400°F/Gas 6, for 20 minutes or until the mushrooms are tender when pierced with a sharp knife and the topping is golden.

6 Serve the mushrooms on plates, garnished with a few frisée salad leaves, drizzled with a little balsamic vinegar.

tips Vegetarians can use 25g pinenuts instead of the bacon.

The mushrooms should be as tasty and succulent as possible for best results, with nice dark gills.

Cooking oil spray is sold in all major supermarkets – one spray from the can contains only approximately 1 calorie and 0.1g fat.

ⓥ crisp potato skins with chilli salsa

These potato skins make a nice lunch snack and are very easy to prepare.

Serves 4 | 180 calories per portion | 1g fat per portion

3 medium washed baking potatoes
(about 275g each)
cooking oil spray
20g sachet fajita seasoning

FOR THE CHILLI SALSA
250g ripe tomatoes, deseeded
and chopped
1 small red onion, finely chopped
1 large mild red chilli, deseeded and
finely chopped
6cm piece of cucumber, deseeded
and finely chopped
juice of 1 lime
salt and black pepper

1 Bake the potatoes in a preheated oven, 200°C/400°F/Gas 6, for 1 hour or until cooked all the way through (see Tip). Remove from the oven and leave until cool enough to handle. Don't turn the oven off.

2 Meanwhile, make the salsa. Put the tomatoes in a bowl with the onion, chilli, cucumber, lime juice and seasoning, stir well, cover and refrigerate.

3 When the potatoes are cool, halve them lengthways and scoop out most of the flesh with a tablespoon, leaving about 0.5cm of flesh still attached to the skin. Cut each skin half into four pieces lengthways so that you have 24 skin wedges altogether.

4 Spray the potato skins well with the cooking oil, then sprinkle the fajita seasoning over them. Place them on a good quality baking tray and bake in the preheated oven for 25 minutes or until the skins are crisp and golden. Serve immediately with the salsa.

serving suggestion Liven up plainly baked fish or chicken with these potato wedges and salsa.

tip Push a metal skewer through the potatoes to hasten cooking.

ⓥ guacamole toasts

This vitamin E-rich snack also makes a good starter, especially before a chilli con carne or tagine.

Serves 4 | 190 calories per portion and 12.5g fat per portion

2 medium tomatoes, peeled, deseeded and chopped (see Tip)

2 small avocados or 1 large, halved, stoned and peeled

1 clove garlic, crushed

1 green chilli, deseeded and very finely chopped

dash of Tabasco (see Tip)

juice of 1 lime

1 small handful fresh coriander, chopped

salt and black pepper

4 slices brown bread from a small loaf, crusts removed

10g vegetarian low-fat spread

4 sprigs of fresh coriander, to garnish

1 Add the tomatoes and avocados to the mixing bowl with the remaining ingredients, except the bread, spread and garnish.

2 Combine the mixture well with a fork until you have a rough purée of dipping consistency, with a few pieces of avocado still apparent.

3 Toast the bread, then halve diagonally and cover with the low-fat spread, then arrange on four serving plates. Top each with a quarter of the avocado mixture and garnish with a coriander sprig.

serving suggestions The guacamole makes a good sandwich filling and there's no need for butter or spread. You could also add prawns or crab and lettuce.

Use the guacamole as a dip with pitta fingers or crudités.

tips Peeling tomatoes may appear quite fiddly, but it really is quite easy – make a cross with a knife on the stalk end of the tomato, place in boiling water for 30 seconds, remove and peel.

Tabasco is a well known brand of chilli sauce but any good chilli sauce will do.

snacks and starters

soups

Home-made soup is a perfect choice for people watching their fat and calorie intake. Flavour and substance come via well-made stocks, vegetables, herbs, spices and seasonings, and there is rarely any need for more than a minimum of added fat.

Soups are so versatile that they can be served as a starter, snack, lunch, packed lunch or main course and, depending on your choice, are good for both summer and winter months. The soups in this chapter reflect this diversity and you will find one suitable for any occasion and for all tastes.

Soups are usually low in cost and easy to make and the following tips will help you produce the best results:

- Use a good quality non-stick frying pan to sauté or sweat your vegetables, if necessary, then transfer them to a heavy-based saucepan for any lengthy cooking that may be required. Alternatively, use a shallow, lidded flameproof casserole (Le Creuset make a perfect one, which will last a lifetime) with sides about 5cm high and you can do the whole job in one pan.

- Invest in a good electric blender with a large goblet, as many soups taste much better if they are all, or part, blended before reheating and serving. This saves having to add thickeners and the puréed ingredients offer a much more powerful flavour.

- Soups are only as good as the quality of their ingredients – so buy the best. I would always go for organic vegetables in my soups as they really do seem to impart a better taste.

carrot and tomato soup

This is definitely a summer or early autumn soup – you need to use good tasty carrots and ripe tomatoes – organic are best.

Serves 4 | 110 calories per portion | 6g fat per portion

1 tbsp olive oil
1 medium onion, finely chopped
200g carrots, finely chopped
1 clove garlic, finely chopped
225g ripe tasty tomatoes (see Tip)
1 tsp ground coriander seeds
(see Tip)
600ml vegetable stock
1 bay leaf
salt and black pepper
1 tbsp dry sherry
4 tbsp half-fat crème fraîche
fresh coriander, to garnish

1 Heat the oil in a large, lidded saucepan and add the onion, carrots and garlic. Stir well and sweat, covered, over a low heat for 15 minutes until softened.

2 Meanwhile, prepare the tomatoes. Make a cross on the stalk end and immerse them in boiling water for 1 minute; remove and peel off the skin, then chop, retaining all the juices.

3 Add the tomatoes to the pan with the ground coriander, stir and simmer for 3 minutes.

4 Add the stock and bay leaf and bring to the boil. Reduce the heat, cover and simmer for 15 minutes, then allow to cool a little and remove the bay leaf.

5 Blend the soup in an electric blender or food processor and return it to the pan to reheat. Season to taste.

6 Add the sherry and crème fraîche and stir through, then serve garnished with coriander.

tips If you can't get any really ripe and tasty fresh tomatoes, use 200g canned peeled plum Italian tomatoes instead.
You can use cumin seeds instead of the coriander.

malaysian crab laksa

A hot and spicy main meal soup. My version is much lower in fat than the traditional one, partly because I have used skimmed coconut milk and less oil. You can reduce the calories and fat even further if you want to (see Tip).

Serves 4 | 360 calories per portion | 15.5g fat per portion

100g rice noodles

1 tbsp groundnut oil

1 quantity of laksa paste (see page 221 or Tip)

400g can coconut milk, skimmed (see Tip)

400ml fish or vegetable stock

400g white and brown crab meat, fresh or frozen (see Tip)

1 tbsp Thai fish sauce (nam pla)

100g fresh beansprouts

1 tbsp each of chopped fresh mint and coriander

1 Cook the noodles according to the pack instructions; drain and set aside.

2 Heat the oil in a large saucepan and sauté the laksa paste for 1–2 minutes, then stir in the coconut milk and stock and bring to a simmer.

3 Add the crab and fish sauce and cook for 1–2 minutes.

4 Stir in the beansprouts and heat for a further 30 seconds or so (the beansprouts should retain their bite), then sprinkle over the chopped herbs, stir through for a few seconds and serve.

tips To reduce the oil content further, use the oil-free laksa paste as described on page 221. The total calories per portion will then be about 300 and the fat content around 9g per portion.

If you don't want to make your own laksa paste, you can buy it ready-made in supermarkets and specialist oriental shops.

You may be able to find ready-skimmed coconut milk in the shops; otherwise, skim your own. Leave a can of full-cream coconut milk to stand for several days. Open it carefully and you will find that the thick fatty coconut cream has risen to the top. Skim this off and discard; use the coconut milk remaining.

You could make a prawn laksa using 400g peeled prawns instead of the crab meat.

wild mushroom soup

This makes a nice change from the 'thick and creamy' type of mushroom soup and is very easy to prepare.

Serves 4 | 170 calories per portion | 7g fat per portion

2 tbsp olive oil

300g chestnut mushrooms, halved

200g wild mushrooms, torn or cut (see Tip)

850ml good quality chicken stock (see Tip)

salt and black pepper

1 large red onion, thinly sliced

2 cloves garlic, chopped

250ml dry white wine

1 tbsp fresh thyme leaves

2 × 25g slices white bread, crusts removed

1 Heat 1 tablespoon of the oil in a large, lidded non-stick frying pan (see Tip) and sauté the mushrooms until the oil has been absorbed, stirring all the time. Add a little stock when the oil has disappeared, reduce the heat and stir for 1 minute more. Season well and transfer the mushrooms to a bowl.

2 Heat another ½ tablespoon of the oil in the pan and sauté the onion and garlic over a medium heat for 10 minutes or until softened, again adding a little stock if necessary.

3 Add the wine and bring to the boil, then reduce the heat and simmer over a medium-low heat for several minutes until everything has softened and amalgamated.

4 Return the mushrooms to the pan, add the rest of the stock and the thyme and simmer, covered, for 10 minutes. Season to taste.

5 While the soup is cooking, brush the bread with the remaining olive oil on one side only. Cut the bread into about 24 squares and place on a solid baking tray. Bake in a preheated oven, 200°C/400°F/Gas 6, for 15 minutes or until golden and crisp.

6 When it is time to serve the soup, garnish with the croûtons.

tips You can buy 'wild' mushrooms in most major supermarkets. For this soup try to get porcini (ceps) and/or chanterelles. Otherwise, you can use all cultivated mushrooms, but try to get tasty varieties – tasteless button mushrooms won't do the trick! Don't use dried mushrooms in this recipe.

Vegetarians can use vegetable stock, although I do find the chicken stock gives a better flavour.

If you don't have a lidded non-stick frying pan, use one without a lid, then transfer the contents of the pan to a lidded saucepan at the end of step 3.

ⓥ panzanella soup

This soup is based on the Italian peasant bread salad, panzanella, and is similar in style to the Spanish gazpacho. It makes a refreshing cold soup as a summer starter.

Serves 4 | 150 calories per portion | 6g fat per portion

400g can peeled plum
Italian tomatoes
½ cucumber, peeled and chopped
1 green pepper, deseeded
and chopped
1 red onion, chopped
2 cloves garlic, crushed
1 tbsp red wine vinegar
1 tbsp fruity olive oil
dash of Tabasco (see Tip)
salt and black pepper
150ml tomato juice
4 slices ciabatta
½ tbsp olive oil

TO GARNISH
6 black stoned olives, finely chopped
8 capers, drained, rinsed and
finely chopped
basil leaves

1 Mix together the first eight soup ingredients, season to taste and blend in an electric blender or food processor until puréed.

2 Add the tomato juice and blend again. Add enough water to make a soup consistency and chill.

3 Brush the ciabatta slices with the oil and bake in a preheated oven, 200°C/400°F/Gas 6, for about 15 minutes until golden and crisp.

4 Meanwhile, mix together the olives and capers.

5 Serve the chilled soup, garnished with the olive mixture and basil leaves, with the ciabatta.

tip Add some chopped fresh chilli instead of the Tabasco.

chilled cucumber soup

Serves 4 | 90 calories per portion | 5.5g fat per portion

1 tbsp sunflower or groundnut oil
(see Tip)
1 medium Spanish onion,
finely chopped
1 organic cucumber (about 450g),
peeled, deseeded and
finely chopped
800ml vegetable stock
salt and white pepper
100ml Greek yogurt
few fresh mint leaves, to garnish

1 Heat the oil in a saucepan and sauté the onion over a medium heat for about 10 minutes, making sure it doesn't colour, until well softened.

2 Stir in the cucumber, stock and seasoning, then bring to the boil. Reduce the heat, cover and simmer for about 15 minutes.

3 Allow the soup to cool a little, then purée in an electric blender or food processor. Transfer to a lidded container, stir in the yogurt and chill until needed.

4 Serve the soup garnished with mint leaves.

tips Olive oil is too strong for this soup – you need a delicate oil such as sunflower or groundnut.

Organic cucumbers have much more flavour, and a denser texture, than non-organic ones.

chickpea soup with lemon

Serves 4 | 190 calories per portion | 8.5g fat per portion

1 tbsp olive oil (see Tip)
15g butter
1 medium Spanish onion,
finely chopped
125g old potatoes, chopped
900ml chicken stock (see Tip)
400g can chickpeas (250g drained
weight), drained and rinsed
juice of 1 lemon
salt and black pepper
chopped fresh parsley, to garnish

1 Heat the oil and butter in a medium-sized lidded saucepan and sauté the onion for at least 10 minutes over a medium heat, until softened.

2 Add the potatoes, stock and chickpeas, stir well and bring to the boil. Reduce the heat, cover and simmer gently for 15 minutes or until the potatoes have softened.

3 Transfer the soup to an electric blender or food processor and blend until smooth.

4 Return the soup to the pan, add the lemon juice and reheat. Season to taste. Serve garnished with the parsley.

serving suggestion Serve the soup with pitta wedges.

tips The soup is very low in saturated fat but, to reduce the saturates even more, you can double the quantity of olive oil and omit the small amount of butter (which does help the velvety texture).
Use fresh chicken stock, if possible, or a good quality cube.
Vegetarians can make the soup with vegetable stock; it is still very good.

ⓥ puy lentil and vegetable winter soup

Serves 4 | 215 calories per portion | 5g fat per portion

1 tbsp olive oil
1 medium onion, finely chopped
2 medium sticks celery, finely chopped
1 clove garlic, finely chopped
1 tbsp Dry Spice Mix (see page 221 or Tip)
2 medium carrots, cut into 1cm chunks
1 medium parsnip, cut into 1cm chunks
1.25 litres vegetable stock
150g Puy lentils (see Tip)
1 tbsp tomato purée
salt and black pepper
chopped fresh parsley, to garnish

1 Heat the oil in a large lidded pan and sauté the onion, celery and garlic for a few minutes until softened. Add the dry spice mix and sauté for another minute.

2 Add the carrots and parsnip, stir for 1 minute, then add the stock, lentils and tomato purée. Stir again and bring to the boil. Reduce the heat, cover and simmer for 30–40 minutes until the lentils and vegetables are tender.

3 Allow the soup to cool a little, then purée half of it in an electric blender or food processor. Return the purée to the pan, stir well into the unblended soup and reheat. Season to taste.

4 Serve the soup garnished with the chopped parsley.

tips Even if you omit the spices, the soup is still very good.
You can use ordinary green or brown lentils instead of the Puy if preferred, but red ones aren't quite so 'meaty'.

ⓥ courgette, bean and pasta soup

Made with typically Italian ingredients, this soup is pretty to look at, and is a simpler version of a minestrone. It makes a hearty lunch or supper.

Serves 4 | 230 calories per portion | 6g fat per portion

1 tbsp olive oil

1 medium red onion, finely chopped

1 stick celery, chopped

1 medium carrot, fairly finely chopped

1 clove garlic, crushed

2 medium courgettes, fairly finely chopped

800ml vegetable stock

400g can chopped tomatoes

salt and black pepper

100g small dried pasta shapes of choice

400g can borlotti beans, drained and rinsed (see Tip)

25g Gruyère cheese, grated

1 tbsp chopped flat-leaf parsley, to garnish

See photograph on page 2.

1 Heat the oil in a large, lidded saucepan and sauté the onion, celery, carrot and garlic for about 15 minutes or until softened and just turning golden.

2 Add the courgettes, stock, tomatoes and a little seasoning, then bring to the boil. Reduce the heat and simmer for about 20 minutes.

3 Add the pasta and beans, and simmer for a further 10 minutes or until the pasta is tender, adding extra stock or water if the soup looks too thick.

4 Check for seasoning, adding more salt and black pepper to taste.

5 Stir in the Gruyère and garnish with the parsley before serving.

tip You can use cannellini beans or a can of mixed beans instead of the borlotti, or omit the beans and add an extra 50g of dried pasta.

chicken noodle soup

A tasty Japanese-style soup, filling enough for a light lunch and yet very low in fat.

Serves 4 | 150 calories per portion | 2g fat per portion

1 litre chicken stock (see Tip)

1 large skinless chicken breast (about 150g)

150g oyster or shiitake mushrooms, sliced

150g pak choi

1½ tbsp miso paste

1 tbsp mirin (rice wine) or medium sherry

100g udon noodles (see Tip)

1 tbsp soy sauce

2 spring onions, finely chopped, to garnish

1 Put the stock and chicken breast into a saucepan and bring to a simmer, then cover and cook for 15 minutes. Remove the chicken and shred into thin strips; return to the pan.

2 Add the mushrooms and pak choi and simmer again for 5 minutes.

3 Combine the miso paste with a little of the hot stock and add this to the pan (see Tip); stir well.

4 Add the mirin or sherry, noodles and soy sauce and simmer for a few minutes.

5 Serve the soup garnished with spring onions.

tips For a more authentic Japanese soup use dashi (dried fish stock) powder sachets instead of the chicken stock – use 40g dashi to 1 litre of water. You could also try a good quality fish stock instead of the chicken stock.

Udon are fat, short Japanese white wheat noodles. If you can't find them, use fine egg thread noodles or rice noodles.

For a hotter note, you could add 1 finely chopped green chilli and a 1cm knob of fresh ginger, peeled and grated, to the soup at step 3.

41

soups

ⓥ middle eastern vegetable soup

This soup has both Moroccan and Turkish flavours and ingredients, and contains plenty of carbohydrate for a satisfying main meal type of soup. It is very easy to make.

Serves 4 | 160 calories per portion | 4.5g fat per portion

1 tbsp olive oil

1 medium Spanish onion, finely chopped

1 tsp harissa (see Tip), or more to taste

2 medium carrots, cut into small dice

2 medium red peppers, deseeded and cut into small squares

1 medium potato, peeled and cut into 1cm dice (see Tip)

50g bulgur wheat

800ml chicken or vegetable stock

salt and black pepper

1 tbsp chopped fresh flat-leaf parsley

juice of ½ lemon

1 Heat the oil in a large, lidded saucepan and sauté the onion over a medium heat until softened and just turning golden. Add the harissa and stir for 1 minute.

2 Add all the vegetables, bulgur wheat and stock, stir and bring to the boil. Reduce the heat, cover and simmer for about 30 minutes, adding a little extra stock or water if you think it needs it.

3 Season to taste and serve the soup with the parsley and lemon juice stirred in.

tips You can buy harissa, a classic Moroccan spicy paste, ready-made in most major supermarkets. Alternatively, there is a simple recipe on page 220.
You can add 75g cooked chickpeas to the soup instead of the potato, if preferred.

⊙ spiced butternut squash soup

This is a creamy and filling soup for an autumn day.

Serves 4 │ 160 calories per portion │ 6.5g fat per portion

800g butternut squash flesh, diced
(see Tip)

2 tbsp olive oil

salt and black pepper

2 cloves garlic, chopped

1 red chilli, deseeded and chopped

1 heaped tsp ground
coriander seeds

1 tsp ground cumin seeds

300ml skimmed milk

600ml vegetable stock

1 In a bowl, toss the squash with half the olive oil and season well. Place the chunks in a roasting pan and roast in a preheated oven, 200°C/400°F/Gas 6, for about 40 minutes or until golden and tender when pierced with a sharp knife.

2 Meanwhile, heat the remaining olive oil in a large non-stick frying pan and sauté the garlic, chilli, coriander and cumin over a medium heat for a few minutes.

3 When the squash is cooked, toss it into the garlic mixture in the pan. Spoon everything into an electric blender or food processor with a little of the milk and blend to a purée.

4 Add the rest of the milk and blend again, then add enough stock to make a soup consistency and blend again for a few seconds. (If your blender isn't large enough you can simply transfer the soup to a saucepan before stirring the stock in thoroughly with a spoon.) Add extra water if the stock doesn't thin the soup enough to suit you.

5 Heat the soup in a saucepan and check the seasoning before serving – it will probably need more salt and black pepper (see Tip).

tips Try different types of squash for this soup, such as Crown Prince or Turks Turban. You need one with a firm, orange flesh, not the insipid Hallowe'en-type pumpkins!

A swirl of half-fat crème fraîche or Greek yogurt added at step 5 will add about 20 calories and 2g fat per portion.

soups

ⓥ red lentil and coriander soup

Many soups containing pulses aren't all that appropriate for summer, but this one, containing red lentils, is quite light and would make a good spring or summer soup with some crusty bread.

Serves 4 │ 250 calories per portion │ 6g fat per portion

1 tbsp groundnut oil

1 large red onion, finely chopped

1 clove garlic, crushed

200g red lentils

1 litre vegetable stock

2 medium carrots, chopped

1 stick celery, chopped

1 red pepper, deseeded and chopped

1 red fresh chilli, deseeded and chopped

1 pack or pot fresh coriander, stalks removed

salt and black pepper

4 tbsp Greek yogurt, to serve (see Tip)

1 Heat the oil in a large, lidded saucepan and sauté the onion for 10–15 minutes until softened, adding the garlic for the last few minutes. Add the lentils, stock, vegetables and chilli, and bring to the boil.

2 Reduce the heat, cover and simmer for 40 minutes or until the lentils are tender. Add half of the coriander to the soup.

3 Allow the soup to cool, then blend in an electric blender or food processor.

4 Return the soup to the pan to reheat and season to taste, then stir in the remaining coriander leaves and the yogurt before serving.

tip You could use half-fat crème fraîche instead of the yogurt.

ⓥ ribollita

Ribollita is a traditional Italian soup or stew, which involves quite a lot of tending. This version is simple and fairly quick but, I feel, still tastes pretty good and is definitely a meal in itself. The soup tastes even better if left overnight and reheated the next day.

Serves 4 | 275 calories per portion | 8g fat per portion

2 tbsp olive oil
2 sticks celery, finely chopped
1 Spanish onion, thinly sliced
1 medium carrot, chopped
1 medium leek, thinly sliced
1 dried chilli, deseeded and chopped
300g spring greens, thinly sliced
(see Tip)
200g potatoes, peeled and cut
into 1cm cubes
200g can chopped tomatoes
1 litre vegetable stock
1 bouquet garni
400g can cannellini beans,
drained and rinsed
salt and black pepper
4 slices ciabatta bread
1 whole clove garlic, peeled

1 Heat the oil in a large, lidded saucepan and add the celery, onion, carrot, leek and chilli. Sauté over a medium heat, stirring, for about 10 minutes or until softened.

2 Add the spring greens, potatoes, tomatoes, stock and bouquet garni to the pan, stir well, then bring to the boil. Reduce the heat, cover and simmer for 20 minutes.

3 Mash half the cannellini beans in a bowl and add to the pan along with the whole beans; bring back to a simmer and cook for 5 minutes. Season to taste.

4 Toast the bread and rub the garlic all across the surface. Put the slices in four soup bowls, then remove the bouquet garni and pour the soup into the bowls.

tips Use the traditional cavalo nero (a very dark coloured cabbage) or Savoy cabbage instead of the spring greens if you prefer.

45

soups

ⓥ red pepper and almond soup

This soup is based on a delicious traditional sauce that you find in Spain served with tuna and other fish.

Serves 4 | 190 calories per portion | 12.5g fat per portion

1 tbsp olive oil

4 red peppers, deseeded and chopped

salt and black pepper

2 cloves garlic, crushed

2 red fresh jalapeño-type chillies, deseeded and finely chopped

20g sun-dried tomato paste

400ml passata

50g ground almonds (see Tip)

1 tbsp red wine vinegar

1 Heat the oil in a large, lidded non-stick frying pan (see Tip) and add the peppers and some seasoning. Stir-fry the peppers over a fairly hot heat for a few minutes until they are tinged golden.

2 Reduce the heat, cover and cook over a low heat for about 20 minutes until softened, adding the garlic, chillies and tomato paste in the last few minutes.

3 Add half the passata, transfer the pan contents to an electric blender or food processor and blend until smooth. Add the rest of the passata and blend again, then add the ground almonds and blend for 10 seconds.

4 Return the mixture to the pan. Add enough water to make a good soup consistency, stir in the vinegar and reheat gently. Check for seasoning, adding salt and pepper to taste.

tips You can use 50g whole blanched almonds – toast them in a non-stick frying pan coated with cooking oil spray, then grind. This gives a greater depth of flavour.

If you don't have a lidded non-stick frying pan, use one without a lid and transfer the pepper mixture to a lidded saucepan after the initial stir-fry.

⊚ vichyssoise

Serves 4 | 145 calories per portion | 4.5g fat per portion

15g butter
600g leeks, chopped
1 medium Spanish onion, chopped
800ml vegetable stock
200g old potatoes, peeled
and chopped
250ml skimmed milk
salt and white pepper (see Tip)
1 tbsp chopped fresh chives,
to garnish

1 Heat the butter in a large saucepan, then add the leeks and onion and stir for 1–2 minutes. Add 2 tablespoons of the stock and stir for a few minutes over a medium heat.

2 Add the potatoes, the rest of the stock and the milk, stir well and bring to the boil. Reduce the heat, cover and simmer for about 30 minutes or until everything is tender.

3 Allow to cool a little, then blend in an electric blender or food processor. You may need to add a little water to thin the soup.

4 Season to taste and reheat the soup (if serving hot) or chill. Serve garnished with the chopped chives.

tip Use white pepper in this soup to avoid dark flecks from black pepper.

⊚ watercress soup

Serves 4 | 150 calories per portion | 2g fat per portion

350g old potatoes, peeled and
cut into small cubes
600ml chicken or vegetable stock
2 bunches of watercress, with large
or tough stalks removed
400ml skimmed milk
2–3 shallots, finely chopped
salt and black pepper
2 tablespoons half-fat crème fraîche

1 Put the potatoes in a lidded saucepan with the stock, most of the watercress, the milk, shallots and a little seasoning. Stir well, then bring to the boil. Reduce the heat, cover and simmer for 20 minutes or until the potatoes are very soft.

2 Allow to cool a little and blend in an electric blender or food processor until smooth. Reheat and add extra seasoning to taste. Stir in the crème fraîche and garnish with the remaining watercress leaves to serve.

tip You need really fresh, dark green watercress for this, and a good quality stock; you can make your own vegetable stock easily (see page 222).

⊽ pea and mint soup

Serves 4 | 140 calories per portion | 3g fat per portion

400g peas, fresh or frozen (see Tips)
1 bunch of spring onions, chopped
1 medium old potato (about 150g),
peeled and cut into small cubes
700ml vegetable stock
1 tbsp chopped fresh mint
pinch of nutmeg
salt and black pepper
2 tbsp half-fat crème fraîche
fresh mint leaves, to garnish

1 Put the peas and spring onions in a lidded saucepan with the potato, stock, mint and nutmeg, then bring to the boil. Reduce the heat, cover and simmer for about 15 minutes or until the peas and potato have softened.

2 Allow to cool a little and blend in an electric blender or food processor.

3 Return the soup to the pan to reheat and season to taste.

4 Serve with the crème fraîche, swirled in, and topped with the mint leaves.

tips You can add the whole trimmed pea pods if you are using mangetout or sugar snap peas (include the pods in the weight) or just include a few of them.

Frozen peas are surprisingly good in this recipe.

grills Most of us are now aware that grilling is one of the healthiest ways to cook meats, poultry, fish and other foods. However, plain grilled foods can err on the side of boring unless you enliven them, which is what this chapter aims to do.

One of the simplest ways to add flavour is to marinate the meat or fish before grilling. A marinade can be as quick and simple as some citrus juice and seasoning, or balsamic vinegar; steeping the food to be grilled in an acid-based marinade for as little as 30 minutes can help add flavour and tenderness. Soy sauce or a ready-made teriyaki marinade are excellent too. You'll find several slightly more elaborate marinades in the recipes that follow, but all are easy and rely mostly on ingredients that you will have in the storecupboard.

Thick, paste-type mixtures, such as harissa or chermoula, can be used to coat meat and fish before grilling for added flavour and depth. Another quick idea is to make a crust, which will often include breadcrumbs mixed with moisteners, herbs and spices.

Plain grills are easy to jazz up with a sauce – vegetable, fruit and low-fat dairy-based sauces and salsas are the answer if you need to say no to traditional, high-fat, dairy-based ones like mayonnaise, béchamel or hollandaise. You will find more ideas for easy low-fat sauces on pages 216–22.

beefburgers with tangy mayonnaise

Beefburgers have an undeserved reputation for being unhealthy and high in fat, but in fact they are rich in minerals and vitamins and can be a fairly low-fat treat, as this recipe shows.

Serves 4 | 245 calories per person | 13.5g fat per portion

450g lean beef, minced (see Tip)

1 small onion (about 100g), very finely chopped

1 egg, beaten

1 dsp dried Herbes de Provence (see Tip)

1 dsp sun-dried tomato paste (see Tip)

salt and black pepper

cooking oil spray

FOR THE MAYONNAISE

2 tbsp good quality mayonnaise

2 tbsp Total Light Greek yogurt

1 dsp capers, rinsed well, dried and chopped

1 tsp Dijon mustard

1 tsp sun-dried tomato paste

1 In a bowl, mix together the beef, onion, egg, herbs and tomato paste and season well. Form into four round burgers, about 1–1.5cm thick.

2 Preheat the grill or a griddle pan and spray the burgers lightly with cooking oil. When the grill or pan is hot, cook the burgers for 4–6 minutes, then turn and cook the other side for about 4 minutes more (see Tip).

3 Meanwhile, mix together the mayonnaise ingredients well in a bowl and season to taste.

4 When the burgers are cooked, serve with the mayonnaise.

serving suggestion Serve the burgers with a green salad and a large burger bun (about 225 calories and 4g fat) or some thick cut oven chips, or a portion of Crisp Potato Skins (see page 30). If using burger buns, fill with sliced gherkins, tomatoes and crisp lettuce as well as some of the mayonnaise. A tomato salsa would also go well.

tips If possible, get a butcher to mince you some rump steak.

If you can't find Herbes de Provence, use ordinary mixed herbs.

Buy sun-dried tomato paste in a jar, not the sort in a tube.

The length of cooking will depend on the exact thickness of the burger and the heat of the grill. The burgers should be well cooked through – slice into one with a sharp knife to make sure there is no sign of pink in the centre before serving.

grills

turkish lamb kebabs

The cumin gives these easy-to-make kebabs a delicious flavour. The marinade would also work with pork.

Serves 4 | 285 calories per person | 16g fat per portion

2 cloves garlic, peeled

1 tsp sea salt

1 tsp ground cumin seeds (see Tip)

½ tsp ground dried chilli

½ tsp black pepper

zest and juice of ½ lemon

1 tbsp olive oil

600g lean lamb (such as leg), cut into bite-sized cubes

1 lemon, cut into wedges

1 small onion (about 100g), quartered and separated into layers

1 Crush the garlic with the salt until it is puréed (a pestle and mortar will do this job well, otherwise use a flat, broad heavy knife and a wooden chopping board).

2 Add the purée to the cumin, chilli, pepper, lemon zest and juice, and oil in a mixing bowl and combine thoroughly, then add the lamb cubes and mix well. Leave to marinate for several hours if possible (see Tip).

3 When ready to cook, preheat the grill. Stir the lemons wedges and onion into the lamb mixture for 1 minute, then thread the lamb, lemon wedges and onion on to four large or eight small kebab sticks, dividing everything up evenly.

4 Put the kebabs on a rack under the hot grill and cook for about 15 minutes, turning halfway through cooking.

serving suggestion This goes very well with the Baba Ganoush with Grilled Red Peppers (see page 68), or you could serve the kebabs with couscous, raita (see following recipe) and a green or tomato salad.

tips Try to buy whole spices and grind them when required (a small coffee bean mill will work well), since the aroma and flavour is much better. Don't keep ground spices for more than a few weeks as they will become stale.

An ideal time to prepare marinades is in the morning before you go to work, so that when you return the marinated ingredients are ready to cook.

lamb koftas with raita

These koftas make a very easy change from burgers – if you don't have any wooden skewers, just grill the meatballs as they are.

Serves 4 | 375 calories per person | 13g fat per portion

400g lean lamb, minced (see Tip)
1 small onion (about 100g),
finely chopped
1 clove garlic, very finely chopped
1.5cm piece of fresh ginger, grated
or very finely chopped (see Tip)
½ tsp each of ground cumin
and coriander
1 tbsp chopped fresh mint (see Tip)
1 egg
salt and black pepper
4 wholewheat pitta breads, to serve
crisp lettuce, such as cos or iceberg,
chopped, to garnish

FOR THE RAITA
100g cucumber, peeled, deseeded
and finely chopped
200ml low-fat natural bio yogurt
1 small clove garlic, crushed
1 dsp chopped fresh mint (see Tip)

1 To make the raita, press out some of the water in the cucumber with kitchen paper. Combine the cucumber with the yogurt, garlic and mint, then season to taste. Cover and leave for the flavours to mingle for 1–2 hours, if possible. Soak eight wooden skewers in water to prevent them burning under the grill.

2 In a mixing bowl, combine the lamb with the onion, garlic, spices, mint, egg and seasoning.

3 When ready to cook, preheat the grill to medium and form the lamb mixture into eight cylindrical shapes around the skewers, leaving one end free for the 'handle'. Grill the koftas for about 15 minutes or until cooked through, turning once or twice.

4 Serve the koftas in the pitta breads with the lettuce and raita.

tips You can make the koftas with lean pork mince, and chopped fresh coriander can be substituted for the mint in both the koftas and the raita.
Fresh ginger will keep for quite a long time if wrapped in kitchen paper and stored in the salad compartment of the fridge.

grills

54

pork satay with peanut sauce

Normally this traditional dish is horrifically high in fat because of the amount of oil and peanuts used. This version still tastes extremely indulgent but is much lower in calories and fat.

Serves 4 | 190 calories per person | 8g fat per portion

400g pork fillet, cut into
bite-sized cubes (see Tip)

4 limes, quartered

FOR THE MARINADE

juice of 1 lime (see Tip)

1 tbsp soy sauce

1 tsp soft dark brown sugar

½ tsp each of ground turmeric,
ground coriander seeds and
ground cumin seeds

1 clove garlic, crushed

2 tbsp skimmed coconut milk
(see Tip, page 34)

salt and black pepper

FOR THE PEANUT SAUCE

2 heaped tbsp Greek yogurt

1 tbsp skimmed milk or
skimmed coconut milk

1½ tbsp peanut butter

dash of Tabasco

1 heaped tsp hot mango chutney

1   Mix together all the marinade ingredients in a mixing bowl and add the pork cubes, stirring thoroughly. Leave to marinate for a few hours, if possible. Soak eight wooden satay sticks in water to prevent them burning when grilled.

2   When ready to cook, preheat the grill and thread the limes on to the satay sticks with the pork cubes.

3   Grill the pork satay for about 12 minutes, turning once and basting from time to time with the marinade.

4   Meanwhile, mix all the peanut sauce ingredients together and season to taste. When the pork is thoroughly cooked, serve with the peanut sauce.

serving suggestion   Serve the satay with Thai fragrant rice or basmati rice and a green salad, or thin strips of carrot, pak choi and fresh beansprouts. Plain boiled rice is about 25 calories per tablespoon and negligible fat.

tips   You can use chicken breast or thigh fillet in this recipe. If using the breast, slice it into 0.5cm thick strips (across the whole length of the breast) and thread on to the satay sticks to form a ripple effect.

You get more juice out of limes if they aren't too green – they are more yellow in colour when ripe. For unripe limes, pierce the skin with a fork or sharp knife and microwave on high for 10 seconds to release more juice.

mustard pork kebabs

Serves 4 | 210 calories per person | 6.5g fat per portion

75ml apple juice

25ml cider vinegar

1 tbsp runny honey

1 tbsp wholegrain Dijon mustard

1 tbsp smooth Dijon mustard

1 tsp dried chopped sage or

2 tsp fresh

salt and black pepper

500g pork fillet (tenderloin), cut into

bite-sized cubes

1 large red dessert apple, halved,

cored and cut into about

20 thin wedges

2 heaped tbsp fromage frais, 8% fat

1 Mix together the apple juice, vinegar, honey, mustards, sage and some seasoning. Arrange the pork cubes in a shallow glass or china bowl and pour the marinade over to coat well. Leave for several hours or preferably overnight.

2 When it is time to cook, preheat the grill to high. Thread the pork cubes on to four flat metal kebab sticks with five apple slices per kebab, evenly spaced.

3 Brush the kebabs with a little more marinade and grill on a rack placed over a grill pan for about 10 minutes, turning once and brushing with more marinade, until the outside is golden and they are cooked through with no pink in the middle.

4 Meanwhile, pour the surplus marinade into a small saucepan and bring to the boil; bubble for 1–2 minutes until reduced to just 1–2 tablespoons of sauce, then remove from the heat and leave to cool slightly. Stir in the fromage frais and serve the sauce with the kebabs.

serving suggestion Serve the kebabs with a mixed leaf salad.

sticky pork spare ribs

Serves 4 | 310 calories per person | 15g fat per portion

1.25kg pork spare ribs, trimmed and

cut into 8–10cm lengths

2cm piece of fresh ginger, grated

2 large cloves garlic, crushed

4 tbsp runny honey (about 60g)

4 tbsp light soy sauce

3 tbsp dry sherry or sake

1 dsp Tabasco

green salad leaves, to garnish

1 Place the spare ribs in a shallow dish.

2 Mix together all the remaining ingredients, except the salad, and pour the mixture over the spare ribs, turning to coat them thoroughly. Leave to marinate for a few hours, if possible, though the spare ribs will still be good even if you don't.

3 Preheat the grill to medium (not too hot or the ribs will burn before they're fully cooked) and grill the ribs on the rack for about 20 minutes, basting from time to time with a little marinade.

4 Meanwhile, pour the marinade into a small saucepan and heat through, bubble well for 1–2 minutes or until you have a thick coating sauce. When the spare ribs are golden and cooked through, remove them from the grill and drizzle the cooked marinade over them.

5 Serve the ribs garnished with salad leaves.

serving suggestion Serve with some plain boiled white rice or rice noodles. Rice is about 25 calories a tablespoon and rice noodles are 225 calories and negligible fat for an average 62.5g (dry weight) serving.

persian chicken kebabs

Serves 4 | 380 calories per person | 12g fat per portion

1 tsp saffron threads

2 tbsp hot water

4 tbsp Greek yogurt (about 100g)

1 tsp ground cumin seeds

1 small onion, very finely chopped (see Tip)

2 cloves garlic, crushed

salt and black pepper

500g chicken breasts, cut into bite-sized cubes

16–20 cherry tomatoes (see Tip)

1 tbsp olive oil

TO SERVE

4 wholewheat pitta breads

100g pack mixed salad leaves

1 lime, cut into 4 wedges

1 In a bowl, mix together the saffron and hot water until the colour starts to run from the threads. Add the yogurt, cumin, onion, garlic and seasoning, mix well and add the cubes of chicken, stirring to combine thoroughly. If possible, leave to marinate for a few hours or even overnight.

2 When ready to cook, preheat the grill to medium. Thread the chicken on to four kebab sticks with the cherry tomatoes, dividing them evenly.

3 Brush the chicken and tomatoes carefully with half the oil, taking care not to brush off the marinade clinging to the meat. Grill for about 5 minutes, then turn, brush again with oil and grill for another 5 minutes or until the chicken is golden and cooked through.

4 Serve with the pitta bread, salad and lime wedges.

tips If you have a food processor, chop the onion for a few seconds until it is virtually puréed. The 'juiced' onion will improve the marinade even more.
  Choose cherry tomatoes that are about the same size as the chicken pieces.

peking duck with pancakes and plum sauce

This is one of my favourite simple dishes as it is high in flavour and contrasting textures, and makes a nice casual supper for friends.

Serves 4 | 375 calories per person | 7.5g fat per portion

4 Gressingham or Barbary duck breasts, skin on

1 tbsp soy sauce

1 tbsp runny honey

1 pack of 20 Chinese pancakes

1 bunch of spring onions, cut into long strips

½ cucumber, halved, deseeded and cut into thin strips

FOR THE SAUCE

400g red plums, stoned and chopped

200ml white wine

50g sugar

2cm piece of fresh ginger, grated

1 cinnamon stick

dash of Tabasco

pinch of salt

1. Put all the sauce ingredients in a saucepan, then bring to the boil. Reduce the heat, cover and simmer for 20 minutes, stirring occasionally, then remove the lid and simmer for a further 20 minutes or until you have a thick, rich sauce. Taste to check the seasoning, remove the cinnamon stick and keep the sauce warm (see Tip).

2. Preheat the grill to medium. Slash the duck breast skins three times diagonally, baste with the soy and honey and grill them for about 15 minutes until just cooked.

3. When the duck is ready, warm the pancakes for a few seconds in the microwave or wrap in foil and warm through in a hot oven for a few minutes. Remove the skin and fat from the duck breasts and slice them into thin pieces.

4. Arrange the duck and vegetables on a platter with the sauce in a bowl in the centre. Serve each person five pancakes and allow them to help themselves to the duck, vegetables and sauce.

tip To save time you could use ready-made plum sauce, available in bottles and jars.

chilli chicken tortillas

Soft flour tortillas are easily obtainable from the ethnic or bread sections of most supermarkets – these filled flatbreads make a great easy supper.

Serves 4 | 315 calories per person | 11.5g fat per portion

1 tbsp olive or groundnut oil

1 medium onion (about 150g), chopped

1 large red pepper, deseeded and cut into thin strips

1 clove garlic, finely chopped

1 red jalapeño chilli, deseeded and finely chopped (see Tip)

juice of ½ lemon

1 dsp runny honey

1 tsp Tabasco

1 tsp sweet paprika, plus extra for sprinkling

300g chicken breast fillets, cut into strips

4 soft flour tortillas, to serve

1 little gem lettuce, cut into thin wedges

FOR THE SAUCE

100ml Greek yogurt

100g cucumber, finely chopped

1 large firm tomato, deseeded and chopped

salt

1 Heat the oil in a non-stick frying pan and sauté the onion and pepper over a medium heat for 5 minutes, stirring from time to time. Add the garlic and chilli and continue to cook for a further 3 minutes.

2 Transfer the contents of the pan to a non-metallic bowl with the lemon juice, honey, Tabasco and paprika; stir well. Add the chicken strips, stirring again, then set aside (if you can leave it to marinate for 1–2 hours, so much the better).

3 When ready to cook, preheat the grill to medium and place the chicken and red pepper strips on the grill pan and brush liberally with the marinade to coat. Cook the chicken for about 4 minutes, turning halfway through cooking.

4 Meanwhile, make the sauce: tip the yogurt into a bowl and add the cucumber, tomato and salt to taste, then stir to combine. Sprinkle some paprika on top.

5 When the chicken and peppers are golden and slightly charred looking, and thoroughly cooked, remove them from the grill. Warm the tortillas under the grill for a few seconds (or warm them in the microwave on defrost or low for 30 seconds or so).

6 Spoon a quarter of the chicken mixture on to each tortilla and top with lettuce and the yogurt mixture; serve with paper napkins (see Tip).

tips Jalapeño chillies are the fairly large, quite plump and slightly pointed chillies that most supermarkets sell. They are not as hot as many types of chilli and have a nice, rounded, sweet heat.

To prevent the filling spilling out, place it in the top half of the tortilla, then fold the bottom half up and roll in the sides.

spicy chicken burgers

These succulent burgers make a great change for the family from ready-made beefburgers, and are very easy to prepare and cook.

Serves 4 | 415 calories per person | 11g fat per portion

3 skinless, boneless chicken breast fillets (400g total weight, see Tip)
1 small onion, very finely chopped
3cm piece of fresh ginger, grated
1 tbsp groundnut oil
1 tbsp soft brown sugar
1 tbsp Thai fish sauce (nam pla)
1 tbsp sherry vinegar (see Tip)

TO SERVE
4 large burger buns
crisp lettuce leaves
1 tbsp half-fat Greek yogurt
2 tbsp sweet mango chutney

1 Lay the chicken fillets flat on a chopping board and, using a sharp knife, cut them into thin 0.5cm escalopes, slicing across the top of the chicken at a slight angle (see Tip). The escalopes will be varying sizes – halve any pieces that look too big to fit into a burger bun. Arrange the chicken in a glass or china shallow bowl.

2 Mix together the next six ingredients and pour the mixture over the chicken slices to coat well. Cover and leave to marinate for several hours or even overnight.

3 When ready to cook, preheat the grill to medium. Place the chicken escalopes over the base of the grill pan (not on the rack), then cook them about 5cm from the heat for 6–8 minutes, turning once, by which time they should be turning slightly golden and cooked through.

4 Meanwhile, slice the burger buns and arrange some lettuce on each base. Beat together the yogurt and chutney. Divide the chicken between the burgers and top with the chutney mixture. Serve immediately.

serving suggestion Serve the burgers with a large green or mixed salad.

tips You may only need two chicken breasts if they are large – 400g will be ample to make four burgers.

If you don't have sherry vinegar, use white wine vinegar instead, or try balsamic vinegar but halve the quantity of sugar.

When slicing the chicken, don't cut vertically down to the board as you might for stir-fries or curries; you want thin slices along the grain.

grills

salmon steaks with a lime and spice crust

Serves 4 | 290 calories per person | 20g fat per portion

2 cloves garlic, peeled

1 tsp sea salt

1.5cm piece of fresh ginger, grated

½ tsp Chinese five spice

½ tsp ground cumin seeds

zest and juice of 1 lime

1½ tbsp groundnut oil

30g fresh breadcrumbs

1 tbsp chopped fresh coriander

4 salmon steaks (about 125g each)

green salad, to serve

1 Crush the garlic with the salt until it is puréed (this is easiest with a pestle and mortar; otherwise use a broad, flat knife blade and a chopping board).

2 Add the spices, lime zest and juice and stir well, then mix in the oil, breadcrumbs and coriander; combine thoroughly.

3 Preheat the grill to high and put a baking tray under the grill to heat.

4 Spoon the crust mixture on to the salmon steaks and smooth it over the tops neatly.

5 Using oven gloves, remove the baking tray from the heat, add the salmon steaks (crust-side up) and return to the grill immediately. Grill for about 6 minutes or until the steaks are cooked to your liking and the crusty top is golden. Serve immediately with a green salad.

tip An even quicker crust can be made using 1½ tablespoons of good quality, ready-made fresh pesto mixed with the breadcrumbs and 1 teaspoon of Tabasco.

grilled king prawns with harissa

Serves 2 | 150 calories per person | 10g fat per portion

1 tbsp Harissa Paste (see page 220)

1 tbsp butter (about 15g)

1 clove garlic, crushed

1 lemon

12 large raw king prawns (about 25g each), peeled and tails left on

1 Mix the harissa paste with the butter and garlic and the juice from a quarter of the lemon. Warm the paste until the butter is very soft and almost melting.

2 Preheat the grill to high. Thread the prawns on to kebab sticks (see Tip), and smother them in the harissa sauce.

3 Grill the prawns for about 2 minutes, then turn and grill for another 2 minutes, basting several times, until they are pink and cooked through. Don't overcook them or they will become tough.

4 Serve the prawns with the remaining lemon cut into 4 wedges.

serving suggestion Plain basmati rice or crusty bread would go well with the prawns, along with a salad of butterhead lettuce and flat-leaf parsley.

tip You can lay the prawns in the base of the grill pan, then grill them. If using metal kebab sticks, get flat ones so that the prawns (or pieces of fish, chicken, or whatever you are cooking) don't roll around in circles when you turn the sticks over halfway through cooking.

seared tuna steaks with lemongrass and chilli

Serves 2 | 285 calories per person | 12.5g fat per portion

1 tbsp light soy sauce (see Tip)
1 tbsp black bean sauce (see Tip)
½ tbsp Thai fish sauce (nam pla)
1 tsp Tabasco
pinch of caster sugar
1 tbsp chopped fresh coriander
1 stalk lemongrass, outer leaves removed and centre finely chopped (see Tip)
2 tuna steaks (about 150g each)
1 dsp sesame oil
green salad, to serve

1 Mix together the first seven ingredients in a shallow, non-metallic bowl, which will fit the tuna steaks nicely.

2 Put the tuna into the bowl and spoon the marinade over the steaks; cover and set aside for 1–2 hours.

3 When you are ready to cook, brush a griddle pan with a little of the oil and heat to very hot. Meanwhile, add the marinade to a small saucepan and bring to the boil and cook until reduced a little.

4 When the griddle is hot, add the tuna steaks and cook for 2 minutes without moving them. Turn and griddle the other side for a further 2 minutes (see Tip).

5 Serve the tuna steaks with the green salad and a dessertspoonful of the heated marinade. Drizzle the rest of the oil over.

tips Light soy sauce is sometimes better in recipes than standard dark soy sauce, and this is one of those occasions in my opinion.

Black bean sauce is available in small jars in most major supermarkets.

If you find a source of fresh lemongrass, buy a few stalks and store the remainder in the freezer.

Don't overcook the tuna or it will dry out – it should still be 'blue' in the centre.

grilled swordfish with chermoula

Chermoula is a Moroccan herb and spice blend used for rubbing into, or marinating, fish and other dishes. There are many different recipes for it, but most contain onion, garlic, chilli, coriander and parsley.

Serves 4 | 285 calories per person | 14g fat per portion

4 swordfish steaks (about 200g each) (see Tip)
1 lemon, cut into wedges and fresh coriander, to garnish

FOR THE CHERMOULA
½ tsp saffron threads
2 tbsp hot water
1 small onion (about 100g), very finely chopped
2 cloves garlic, crushed
1 fresh red chilli, deseeded and finely chopped
1 tsp sweet paprika
½ tsp ground cumin seeds
1 tsp Tabasco
2 tbsp chopped fresh flat-leaf parsley
2 tbsp chopped fresh coriander
juice of 1 lemon
2 tbsp olive oil
salt and black pepper

1 First make the chermoula. In a bowl, steep the saffron threads in the hot water until their colour starts to run.

2 Add the remaining chermoula ingredients to the bowl and combine well (see Tip).

3 Place the swordfish steaks in a shallow bowl and spoon the chermoula mixture over them, rubbing it in well. If possible, leave to marinate for at least 1 hour (see Tip).

4 When ready to cook, preheat the grill to high. Grill the swordfish for about 2 minutes each side, or until just cooked through. Garnish with lemon wedges and whole coriander leaves.

serving suggestion Couscous, enriched with small pieces of chopped dried apricots or sultanas, would go well with this, along with some robust salad leaves.

tips Pregnant women shouldn't eat swordfish.
Blend the marinade ingredients together in an electric blender in step 2.
For a change, you could cube the swordfish steaks and thread the pieces on to kebab sticks before grilling.

salmon teriyaki

Even on a low-fat diet, you should eat some salmon (and other oily fish) because of the beneficial omega-3 oils. Here is a simple yet tasty way to serve it.

Serves 2 | 320 calories per person | 18g fat per portion

2 tsp caster sugar
1.5cm piece of fresh ginger, grated
2 tbsp soy sauce (see Tip)
1 tbsp mirin (see Tip)
1 tbsp dry sherry or sake (see Tip)
2 salmon fillets (about 150g each), skin on
cooking oil spray (optional)

1 Mix together the first five ingredients in a bowl. Place the salmon fillets in a small shallow bowl, pour the marinade over and leave for a few hours, turning once or twice, if possible.

2 Preheat the grill to high. Pat the salmon dry and lay it, flesh-side up, on the very hot grill rack (or place on a griddle, sprayed with cooking oil, flesh-side down) and cook without moving them for about 3 minutes. Turn the fillets over, baste with some of the marinade, and cook for another 2 minutes or until they are cooked to your liking and the skin is golden.

3 Meanwhile, put the marinade in a small saucepan and boil it for 1–2 minutes until thickened.

4 Serve the fillets with some of the marinade poured over.

serving suggestion Serve the salmon with chopped pak choi, stir-fried in groundnut oil with sesame seeds, or with steamed spinach and a few tablespoons of plainly cooked rice, or egg thread or rice noodles.

tips Buy good quality soy sauce – Kikkoman is one of the best makes.
Mirin is a sweet Japanese alcoholic rice wine used in cooking, which is available in some supermarkets, specialist food shops and Japanese food shops, as well as by mail order or on the internet.
Sake is a dry Japanese rice wine often used as an aperitif and also in cooking. It is quite widely available.

grills

ⓥ grilled summer vegetables with couscous

This is a colourful and light dish for warm evenings – you could even grill the vegetables on the barbecue.

Serves 2 | 335 calories per person | 9.5g fat per portion

2 red onions (about 200g), quartered

1 bulb fennel (about 100g), and cut into 0.5cm slices

2 medium courgettes, cut diagonally into 3mm slices

1 large yellow pepper, quartered and deseeded

2 large ripe tomatoes, quartered

8 asparagus spears, woody stems removed (see Tip)

1 tbsp olive oil

1 dsp balsamic vinegar, plus extra for drizzling (optional)

salt and black pepper

4 black stoned olives, halved

handful of fresh basil leaves, to garnish

FOR THE COUSCOUS

100g couscous

250ml hot vegetable stock

5cm piece of cucumber, halved, deseeded and chopped

1 firm ripe tomato, deseeded and finely chopped

1 Blanch the onions and fennel in boiling water for 2 minutes; add the courgettes and pepper and blanch for a further 2 minutes. Drain immediately and tip the vegetables into a large mixing bowl with the tomatoes and asparagus.

2 Mix together the oil and vinegar with plenty of seasoning and add to the vegetables. When they are cool enough to handle, mix everything well, using your hands, so that all the vegetables have a coating of the dressing.

3 Preheat the grill to medium. Tip the vegetables into the grill pan (or a shallow baking tray) and arrange them in a single layer and put the pan under the grill.

4 Cook for about 15 minutes, turning the vegetables every few minutes, until softened and golden and beginning to char at the edges (see Tip). Season again before serving.

5 Meanwhile, reconstitute the couscous in the boiling vegetable stock in a bowl. When the couscous is ready, stir the cucumber and tomato into it.

6 Arrange the couscous on plates with the grilled vegetables and olives on top, then garnish with basil and a little drizzling of vinegar, if you like.

tips You can easily tell where to break the woody stems from the asparagus. Hold one end of the asparagus spear between each forefinger and thumb and snap – the stem will break where the woodiness begins – discard the paler woody end and retain the green tip.

If the vegetables dry out before they are cooked, sprinkle a little vegetable stock or water over them.

You could crumble some feta cheese over the top of the vegetables before serving; this would add about 62 calories and 5g fat per 25g serving. Incidentally, black olives contain about 3 calories and 0.3g fat each.

spicy bean burgers

*Bean burgers have an unfortunate profile – a sandal-wearing, health-food freaks
kind of connotation – and that's a shame, as they can be really delicious. Try these!*

Serves 4 | 205 calories per person | 5g fat per portion

100g quick-cook brown rice

1 small onion (about 100g),
very finely chopped

400g can cooked red kidney
beans, drained

1 clove garlic, crushed

1 tsp Harissa Paste (see page 220
or Tip)

1 dsp tomato chutney

1 tsp sun-dried tomato paste

salt and black pepper

1 tbsp polenta

1 tbsp olive oil

1 Cook the rice in boiling salted water with the onion for 12 minutes or
according to the pack instructions; drain and set aside.

2 Meanwhile, mash the beans in a mixing bowl with the garlic, harissa,
chutney, tomato paste and seasoning to combine well.

3 When the rice is cooked and cooled a little, add it to the bowl and
mix very thoroughly, then form into four patties.

4 Sprinkle the polenta on to a large plate and coat each side of
the burgers.

5 When ready to cook, preheat the grill to medium. Brush the burgers
well with the olive oil and cook for 2–3 minutes each side until golden
and hot right through. Serve immediately.

serving suggestion Serve the burgers in wholemeal buns with a
tomato salsa or relish and a green side salad.

tip If you don't want to make your own harissa paste for this recipe, buy it
in small jars in supermarkets.

grills

ⓥ baba ganoush with grilled red peppers

This is a great-tasting warm side salad, ideal with any grilled, barbecued or roast lamb or chicken dish. Baba ganoush is a Middle Eastern purée based on aubergine and is delicious.

Serves 4 | 135 calories per person | 9g fat per portion

2 red peppers (about 200g total weight), halved and deseeded

4 small aubergines (about 300g total weight), pricked all over

20g pinenuts

1 clove garlic, crushed

juice of ½ lemon

1 tbsp olive oil

sea salt and black pepper

200ml Total Light Greek yogurt at room temperature

2 tbsp vegetable stock (see Tip)

1 Preheat the grill to medium. Place the peppers, skin-side up, and the aubergines on a rack under the grill (see Tip).

2 Cook them for about 20 minutes, turning the aubergines occasionally, until the pepper skins have charred and the aubergines are charred on the outside and soft inside – test them with a sharp knife to make sure.

3 In the meantime, heat a small non-stick frying pan and dry-fry the pinenuts until they begin to brown (watch them carefully as once they start to brown, they can quickly burn). Take off the heat and reserve.

4 Allow the vegetables to cool until you can handle them, then peel off the pepper skins (over a bowl, so that you retain any juices) and remove the flesh from the aubergines with a spoon and roughly chop.

5 Put the aubergine flesh in a bowl and mix it with the garlic, lemon juice, oil and seasoning. Arrange the aubergine mixture on four side plates.

6 Cut up the peppers with kitchen scissors (over the bowl with the juices in) then sprinkle them, plus the juices, over the aubergine. Grind some sea salt over the top.

7 Combine the yogurt with the vegetable stock and check the seasoning. Pour the mixture over the aubergine and peppers, then scatter the pinenuts on top. When you serve the salad, it should still be slightly warm.

serving suggestion Try serving this salad with the Turkish Lamb Kebabs (see page 52). You could also use the salad to fill pitta or flatbreads with some plain grilled sliced chicken.

tips If serving the salad with roast or grilled meat, mix any meat juices into the yogurt, instead of (or as well as) the vegetable stock, to make 2 tablespoons altogether.

The vegetables can be baked in the oven, 200°C/400°F/Gas 6 for about 45 minutes, instead.

casseroles, braises and stews

This chapter contains twenty-four great ideas for healthy one-pot meals. Some of the dishes take longer to cook than you may be used to, but on the other hand most of the cooking time doesn't need you to be there and the preparation is almost always extremely easy, even for novice cooks.

Casseroles and stews are ideal family fare – hungry, non-waist-watching members of the household won't even realise that these recipes are low in fat as they are high on flavour and substance, but you can always give them extra carbohydrates, such as potatoes or pasta, if needed.

I have concentrated on giving you low-fat versions of traditional, much-loved, world-wide favourites, such as chilli, goulash, tagines, cassoulet, curries and coq au vin – those types of dishes that we all long to eat now and then but which are usually so high in fat that we feel guilty if we do – no longer!

Casseroles are an ideal way to cook low-fat cuts of meat, and also game, which is usually low in fat, as the meat is less inclined to dry out. Lastly, one-pot meals can be bulked out with plenty of vegetables and pulses to add both flavour and fibre, and are the best winter cooking method for vegetarian meals.

When slow-cooking, it helps if you have a very good quality heavy-based flameproof casserole pan with a tight-fitting lid for more consistent results. A flameproof pan also means that you needn't transfer sautéd or sweated ingredients from a frying pan to the casserole, but can do both steps in the one pan.

beef bourguignon

The classic French red wine stew can be low in fat as long as you choose a lean cut of braising steak and add lean bacon rather than streaky.

Serves 4 | 295 calories per portion | 10.5g fat per portion

cooking oil spray

100g extra-lean back bacon, cut into strips

1 tbsp olive oil

500g lean braising steak, trimmed and cut into bite-sized cubes

16 small shallots or 12 larger ones (about 250g total weight)

1 clove garlic, crushed (see Tip)

1 tbsp plain flour

200ml red wine

100ml beef stock

bouquet garni

salt and black pepper

125g small mushrooms

1 tbsp chopped fresh parsley

1 Heat a flameproof casserole (see Tip), coat lightly with cooking oil spray and fry the bacon until golden; set aside.

2 Add half the olive oil to the pan and brown the steak over a high heat, remove and reserve.

3 Add the rest of the oil and the shallots to the pan and brown them, turning frequently.

4 Add the garlic, flour, wine, stock, bouquet garni and seasoning, stir well, bring to a simmer, cover and transfer to a preheated oven, 170°C/335°F/Gas 3½, and cook for 2 hours (see Tip).

5 Add the mushrooms and half the parsley, remove the bouquet garni and cook for a further 30 minutes, then serve garnished with the remaining parsley.

serving suggestion Serve with green vegetables and mashed potato.

tips You can buy jars of good quality, ready-minced garlic, which can be used in this recipe and many others in this book.

If you don't have a flameproof casserole, cook the bacon and brown the meat and onions in a good quality non-stick frying pan, then transfer them to a casserole dish and proceed with Step 5.

You can cook this dish on the hob, although make sure it simmers very gently – buy a heat diffuser mat from a cookstore, if your hob doesn't simmer low enough.

carbonnade of beef

A simple casserole which depends for its flavour on good quality beef, plenty of onions and stout or beer.

Serves 4 │ 325 calories per portion │ 11.5g fat per portion

cooking oil spray

500g lean braising steak, trimmed and cut into 6 × 5cm 'mini' steaks

2 tbsp olive oil

2 large onions (about 500g total weight), sliced

2 cloves garlic, crushed (see Tip)

1 tbsp brown sugar

1 tbsp plain flour

500ml stout (see Tip)

1 beef stock cube, crumbled

1 tbsp tomato purée

1 bay leaf

salt and pepper

1 tbsp chopped fresh parsley, to garnish

1 Spray a large, shallow non-stick frying pan with a little cooking oil, heat until hot and brown the meat on all sides, then transfer it to a casserole dish.

2 Add the olive oil to the pan and sauté the onions over a medium heat for about 10 minutes, or until they begin to soften. Add the garlic and sugar to the pan, stir well, reduce the heat to medium-low and cook for another 10 minutes or until the onions start to caramelise.

3 Stir in the flour and cook for 1 minute, then add the stout, stock cube and tomato purée, stir well and bring to a simmer.

4 Transfer the onion mixture to the casserole dish and mix with the beef. Add the bay leaf and plenty of seasoning, cover and cook in a preheated oven, 170°C/335°F/Gas 3½, for 2 hours.

5 Check the seasoning, remove the bay leaf and serve garnished with the parsley.

serving suggestion Boiled potatoes, dark green cabbage and carrots are delicious with the beef.

tips Garlic is used in many casseroles as it brings out the flavours without leaving a noticeably garlicky taste.

For a less rich stew, you could use ordinary beer instead of stout.

71

casseroles, braises and stews

beef and winter vegetable hotpot

Hotpot is a traditional British dish, which is easily turned into a high protein, low-fat family supper.

Serves 4 | 410 calories per portion | 13g fat per portion

2 tbsp olive oil

400g lean braising steak, trimmed and cut into bite-sized cubes

1 large onion (about 200g), sliced

1 large leek (about 150g), sliced

2 sticks celery, chopped

1 large carrot, sliced into rounds

1 rounded tbsp plain flour

450ml beef stock

1 tsp mixed dried herbs

salt and black pepper

400g can borlotti beans, drained and rinsed (see Tip)

500g old potatoes, peeled and sliced into 0.5cm rounds

2 tbsp grated fresh Parmesan cheese (see Tip)

1 Heat half the oil in a large non-stick frying pan and brown the beef on all sides over a high heat, then remove with a slotted spoon and reserve.

2 Add the rest of the oil to the pan with the onion and sauté for 5 minutes over a medium-high heat, stirring frequently, until softened. Add the leek, celery and carrot, and cook for another 3–4 minutes, stirring.

3 Add the flour and stir for a minute, then pour in the stock, herbs and seasoning, stir well and bring to a simmer.

4 Return the meat to the pan with the beans and stir well.

5 Arrange half the potato slices in the base of a casserole dish and tip the meat mixture in, smoothing it down evenly. Top with the remaining potato slices, cover and cook in a preheated oven, 170°C/335°F/ Gas 3½, for 1½ hours.

6 Remove the lid, sprinkle the cheese over the top and cook, uncovered, for a further 30 minutes until the top is brown and the potatoes and meat are tender.

serving suggestion This is a meal in itself but you could serve it with a green vegetable, such as green beans or broccoli.

tips Any ready-cooked pulses can be used instead of the borlotti beans – try cannellini beans, red kidney beans or brown lentils.

Use fresh Parmesan and grate it yourself – it's much tastier than the ready-grated kind in tubs. The cheese will keep, wrapped in greaseproof paper, in the fridge for several weeks, or you could grate the whole lot and freeze the remainder in a lidded container.

chilli con carne

Most people love chilli – this one is medium-hot, but simply by adjusting the amount of Tabasco that is used, you can easily make it milder or extra hot.

Serves 4 | 285 calories per portion | 9.5g fat per portion

1½ tbsp groundnut oil

400g lean braising steak, trimmed and cut into 1cm cubes

1 large Spanish onion, peeled and finely chopped

1 large red pepper, deseeded and cut into 1cm squares

1 clove garlic, crushed

2 fresh red jalapeño chillies, chopped (see Tip)

1 tsp Tabasco (see Tip)

1 tsp each ground cumin and sweet paprika

400g can chopped tomatoes

1 tbsp tomato purée

400g can red kidney beans, drained and rinsed

250ml beef stock

salt and black pepper

good handful fresh coriander, to serve

1 Heat half the oil in a large, lidded non-stick frying pan and brown the meat over a high heat, stirring frequently. Remove the meat from the pan with a slotted spoon and reserve.

2 Add the rest of the oil with the onion, pepper, garlic and chillies and sauté, stirring occasionally, for 10 minutes. Add the Tabasco, cumin and paprika and stir for another minute.

3 Pour in the tomatoes, tomato purée, beans, stock and seasoning, stir well and bring to a simmer, then return the meat to the pan and combine well. Taste for 'hotness' and adjust as necessary (see Tips).

4 Cover and simmer gently for 1–1½ hours or until the sauce is a rich colour and everything is tender. Check the seasoning and stir in plenty of fresh coriander before serving.

serving suggestion Serve with rice or a baked potato, Chilli Salsa (see page 30), and 1 tablespoon half-fat crème fraîche per person (adds 2.2g fat per portion) or light Greek yogurt (adds 0.7g per portion).

tips Jalapeño chillies are quite mild, but will be hotter if you add the seeds to the pan with the flesh, or you could choose hotter chillies such as bird's eye.

1 teaspoon Tabasco will give a mild heat – add 2 or 3 teaspoons to make the chilli hotter.

The heat of the dish increases as it cooks, so when you taste for heat before the final cooking, remember this.

You can cook the chilli in the oven; transfer everything to a casserole dish at the end of step 3.

73

casseroles, braises and stews

hungarian goulash

A rich and flavoursome casserole that even young children seem to enjoy.

Serves 4 | 295 calories per portion | 14g fat per portion

1½ tbsp groundnut oil

450g lean braising steak, trimmed and cut into bite-sized cubes

1 large onion, finely chopped

2 tbsp sweet Hungarian paprika, plus extra to garnish (see Tip)

1 tbsp plain flour

1 tsp caraway seeds

400g can plum tomatoes

200ml beef stock

1 small glass red wine

salt and pepper

400g old floury potatoes, peeled and cubed

2 small or 1 large red pepper, deseeded and sliced

100ml half-fat crème fraîche

1 Heat half the oil in a large, lidded non-stick frying pan and brown the meat over a high heat. Remove the steak from the pan with a slotted spoon and reserve.

2 Add the rest of the oil and sauté the onion over a medium-high heat for about 10 minutes, stirring occasionally.

3 Add the paprika and flour, stir and cook for a minute, then add the caraway, tomatoes, stock, wine and seasoning, return the meat to the pan, stir well and bring to a simmer (see Tip).

4 Cover and simmer gently for 1½ hours. Add the potatoes to the casserole with the pepper and stir well, then cook for a further 30 minutes until everything is tender.

5 Check the seasoning, stir in the crème fraîche and serve, garnished with paprika.

serving suggestion As the dish contains potatoes, you may need only a green salad or perhaps some white cabbage, but hungry family members may like to eat the goulash with plain boiled rice or egg thread noodles or pasta shapes.

tips There are various types of paprika in the shops – make sure you get good quality Hungarian paprika, which is quite mild and sweet. If you use hot paprika, the dish will probably be inedible!

You can cook the casserole in a preheated oven, 170°C/335°F/Gas 3½, in which case transfer the mixture to the casserole at the end of step 3.

gascony lamb crumble

A simple, crunchy-topped casserole with a great depth of flavour due to the red wine and anchovies.

Serves 4 | 395 calories per portion | 16.5g fat per portion

1 tbsp olive oil

500g lean lamb fillet, cut into small cubes

1 medium onion, roughly chopped

150g celeriac, finely chopped

3 cloves garlic, crushed

200ml red wine

125ml lamb stock

400g can cannellini beans, drained and rinsed

4 anchovy fillets, rinsed well and chopped (see Tip)

1 dsp tomato purée

black pepper

60g good quality white bread, roughly crumbled or chopped into small pieces

cooking oil spray

1 Heat half the oil in a non-stick frying pan and cook the lamb pieces in two batches over a high heat until brown on all sides. Remove with a slotted spoon and transfer to a fairly shallow, family-sized earthenware-type casserole dish.

2 Heat the remaining oil and sauté the onion and celeriac over a medium heat for 10 minutes until softened. Add the garlic and stir for another minute, then transfer to the casserole dish.

3 Heat the wine and stock in the frying pan and add this with the beans, anchovies and tomato purée to the casserole and stir well, mashing some of the beans with a fork as you do so.

4 Season with pepper, cover and cook in a preheated oven, 170°C/335°F/Gas 3½, for 1½ hours. Check the seasoning – the casserole is unlikely to need extra salt as the anchovies are salty.

5 Preheat the grill to hot (see Tip). Sprinkle the bread evenly over the top of the casserole, then spray with the cooking oil, and grill until the bread is golden and crispy. Serve immediately.

serving suggestion New or mashed potatoes or French bread and green beans or a salad are ideal with this dish.

tips Anchovies add a lot to the fine flavour of this casserole but you won't detect a 'fishy' smell or flavour, so try not to leave them out.

Two tablespoons (50ml) of half-fat crème fraîche can be stirred into the casserole before topping with the bread, which would add 20 calories and 2g fat per portion.

casseroles, braises and stews

lamb tagine with chickpeas

This is a sweet and aromatic spiced stew from Morocco – I've cut some corners to make it a fairly quick and easy dish to prepare.

Serves 4 | 400 calories per portion | 18g fat per portion

1 tbsp olive oil

600g lean lamb fillet (neck or leg), cubed

1 onion, sliced

2 cloves garlic, peeled

1 tsp ground cinnamon

2cm piece of fresh ginger, chopped

1 dsp ground coriander

1 tsp ground cumin

1 sachet saffron mixed with 1 tbsp hot water

1 level tbsp chopped fresh parsley

1 level tbsp chopped fresh coriander

400g can chickpeas, drained and rinsed

50g ready-to-eat stoned prunes, halved

50g ready-to-eat dried apricots, halved

400ml lamb stock

salt and black pepper

1 Heat the oil in a flameproof casserole or good quality, lidded frying pan and brown the lamb over a high heat, turning once or twice until browned all over. Reduce the heat to medium.

2 Meanwhile, purée the onion, garlic, cinnamon, ginger, coriander, cumin and saffron plus water, and half the fresh herbs, in an electric blender or, if you don't have one, chop the onion as finely as you can and mash well with the spices and herbs in a bowl (see Tip).

3 Add this mixture to the lamb and stir well for 1–2 minutes, then add the chickpeas, dried fruits, stock and plenty of seasoning and stir again. Bring to a simmer, cover and cook for 1½ hours (see Tip).

4 Check the seasoning, sprinkle with the remaining parsley and coriander, then serve (see Tip).

serving suggestion Serve with couscous, either plain or jazzed up with some chopped tomato, cucumber, raisins and, if you like, 20g toasted pinenuts, which would add 3.5g fat per portion.

tips For a change, make little lamb meatballs – mince the lamb with half the spices and form into small balls before browning, then blend the onion with the remaining spices and half the herbs and proceed as above.

If using a flameproof casserole, you could oven-cook the tagine at 170°C/335°F/Gas 3½, instead of simmering it on the hob.

The tagine looks nice garnished with a few toasted flaked almonds – 25g almonds (in total) would add around 3.5g fat per portion but virtually no saturated fat.

lamb rogan josh

This is a fairly hot lamb curry, ideal for the winter months.

Serves 4 | 320 calories per portion | 18g fat per portion

1½ tbsp groundnut oil
600g lean lamb fillet, cubed
2 medium onions, sliced
2 cloves garlic, crushed
1 tsp cardamom seeds (see Tip)
1 tsp ground cinnamon
1 tsp ground coriander
1 heaped tbsp sweet paprika
1 tsp hot chilli powder (see Tip)
1 tbsp tomato purée
100ml good meat stock
salt and black pepper

1 Heat half the oil in a lidded non-stick frying pan or flameproof casserole and brown the lamb over a high heat, turning once or twice until browned all over. Remove the meat with a slotted spoon and reserve.

2 Heat the rest of the oil and sauté the onions over a medium-high heat, stirring frequently, until softened and turning golden.

3 Add the garlic, cardamom, cinnamon and coriander to the pan, and stir for 1–2 minutes.

4 Add the paprika and chilli powder, and stir for another minute, adding a little stock if necessary, before returning the meat to the pan.

5 Add the tomato purée and the stock plus some seasoning, stir well and bring to the boil. Reduce the heat, cover, and simmer gently for 1 hour, or until the meat is tender and you have a rich red sauce.

serving suggestion Basmati rice and a cucumber and low-fat natural bio yogurt salad are ideal with this curry.

tips You may need to buy cardamom pods, which should be split open to remove the seeds inside.
You can add extra chilli powder to taste, or 1–2 teaspoons of Tabasco.

casseroles, braises and stews

greek lamb with lemons and feta

This gorgeous, light lemony casserole is a great late summer supper.

Serves 4 | 400 calories per portion | 17g fat per portion

½ tbsp olive oil

500g lamb fillet, cubed

12 shallots, peeled

2 cloves garlic, crushed

400g ripe fresh tomatoes, roughly chopped

zest and juice of 1 lemon

400ml lamb stock (see Tip)

salt and pepper

450g Charlotte new potatoes (or other well-flavoured new potatoes), cut into bite-sized pieces as necessary

2 tbsp chopped fresh parsley

80g feta cheese, crumbled

1 lemon, cut into 4 wedges, to serve

1 Heat the oil in a good quality, large, lidded non-stick frying pan, add the lamb and shallots and cook over a high heat for 8 minutes, turning occasionally, until the meat has browned on all sides (see Tip) and the shallots are tinged with gold.

2 Add the garlic, tomatoes, lemon juice and zest, stock and seasoning, stir well and bring to the boil (see Tip).

3 Reduce the heat, cover and cook for 1½ hours, then mix in the potatoes and cook for another 30 minutes or until they are tender.

4 Check the seasoning, stir in the parsley and feta cheese, and serve with the lemon wedges.

serving suggestion This can be eaten on its own or with a green salad and some rustic bread to dip in, as there are plenty of juices to mop up.

tips If you can't get lamb stock, a vegetable stock made from Marigold bouillon powder is quite good in this dish.

In step 1, leave the lamb without turning it for the first couple of minutes, so that the underside has time to seal and not stick, then do the same on the other sides.

You can cook the dish in the oven: transfer everything to a casserole dish at the end of step 2.

pork and apricot casserole

Pork marries very well with dried fruits, and this casserole is good for using storecupboard ingredients.

Serves 4 | 330 calories per portion | 8.5g fat per portion

100g ready-to-eat dried apricots, roughly chopped
50g dried apples, roughly chopped
50g ready-to-eat stoned prunes, roughly chopped
150ml dry white wine
500g pork fillet, cut into bite-sized cubes
1 tbsp plain flour
1 tbsp olive oil
1 medium onion, roughly chopped
2 whole cloves
1 tsp ground cinnamon (see Tip)
150ml chicken stock
salt and pepper

1 Soak all the fruits in the wine, adding water to cover, if necessary, for 30 minutes.

2 Dredge the pork in the flour. Heat the oil in a good quality, lidded non-stick frying pan or flameproof casserole and sauté the onion and pork over a medium-high heat, stirring frequently, until the meat is browned all over.

3 Add the spices and any remaining flour and stir well, then add the soaked dried fruits and wine, stock and seasoning; stir well to combine. Bring to the boil, adding a little extra water or stock if the mixture looks too thick.

4 Reduce the heat, cover and simmer gently for 1¼ hours or until everything is tender. Check the seasoning and remove the cloves before serving.

serving suggestion Serve with cabbage, green beans and boiled potatoes.

tip You can use a whole cinnamon stick instead of the ground variety, if preferred, but remove it before serving.

chicken dopiaza

Dopiaza is a spiced chicken dish containing lots of onion – if you have a good spice storecupboard, it is an easy curry to make.

Serves 4 | 420 calories per portion | 15.5g fat per portion

4 onions (500g total weight), sliced

3 cloves garlic, halved

3cm piece of fresh ginger, chopped

1 tsp each of ground chilli, cinnamon, cardamom seeds, black pepper and turmeric (see Tip)

4 cloves

2 fresh chillies, halved (see Tip)

1½ tbsp groundnut oil

8 skinless, boneless chicken thighs (800g total weight)

2 fresh tomatoes

1 tsp sugar

400g cooked potatoes

salt

1 tsp garam masala

200ml full-fat natural yogurt

sprigs of fresh coriander, to garnish

1 Purée half the onions in an electric blender with the garlic, ginger, spices and chillies.

2 Heat half the oil in a lidded non-stick frying pan and cook the chicken over a high heat in two batches, until browned all over. Remove with a slotted spoon and reserve.

3 Heat the rest of the oil and sauté the remaining onions over a medium-high heat for about 10 minutes until softened and quite golden. Add a little water if the onions become too dry.

4 Add the puréed onion mixture to the pan and cook for 1–2 minutes, stirring.

5 Reduce the heat a little and add the tomatoes, sugar, potatoes, salt and a little water (about 50ml). Return the chicken to the pan with any juices, stir and bring to the boil. Reduce the heat, cover and simmer for 40 minutes or until the chicken is cooked through.

6 Stir in the garam masala and the yogurt, and simmer for 2 minutes, then serve garnished with coriander.

serving suggestion A green salad and mango chutney are all you need with this curry, although hungry diners can add some basmati rice too.

tips Don't keep ready-ground spices for longer than a few weeks and always store in a cool, dark place; they soon lose their aroma and flavour and aren't worth using.

If you retain the seeds of the fresh chillies, the hotter the curry. Different varieties of chilli also have varying levels of heat – most supermarkets provide guidelines on their packs.

casseroles, braises and stews

chicken cacciatore

This easy Italian casserole is colourful and full of gutsy flavours.

Serves 4 | 320 calories per portion | 15g fat per portion

1 tbsp olive oil

8 skinless, boneless chicken thighs (about 800g total weight)

1 red pepper, deseeded and chopped into 1cm squares

4 cloves garlic, crushed

1 dsp sun-dried tomato paste (see Tip)

200ml dry white wine

400g can chopped Italian tomatoes

1 tbsp chopped fresh mixed herbs (see Tip)

salt and black pepper

16 black stoned olives

12 capers, rinsed and dried

1 Heat the oil in a large, lidded non-stick frying pan or flameproof casserole and brown the chicken over a high heat for a few minutes, turning occasionally. Remove from the pan with a slotted spoon and reserve.

2 Add the pepper and sauté for a few minutes over a medium-high heat until softened and golden, then add the garlic and stir for another minute.

3 Add the tomato paste, wine, tomatoes, half the herbs, and seasoning, mix everything well and return the chicken to the pan. Bring to the boil.

4 Reduce the heat to low, cover and simmer for 40 minutes or until everything is tender and the chicken is cooked through (see Tip).

5 Stir in the remaining herbs, and the olives and capers, then serve.

serving suggestion Pasta or rice and a green salad or green beans are ideal with the casserole.

tips Buy a good quality sun-dried tomato paste in a jar, not the kind in tubes.
For the fresh mixed herbs, try thyme, rosemary and oregano, or you could use thyme, basil and parsley.
If cooking the dish in a flameproof casserole, you can oven-cook it at 180°C/350°F/Gas 4, for 50 minutes, if preferred.

casseroles, braises and stews

creamy chicken casserole

This is a nice winter casserole for the family – it tastes quite mild and creamy but does have a kick to it, because of the Dijon mustard.

Serves 4 | 315 calories per portion | 13g fat per portion

1 tbsp groundnut oil

8 skinless, boneless chicken thighs (800g total weight)

16 small shallots or 8 large ones, peeled

400ml chicken stock

250g carrots, sliced

2 leeks, sliced

1 tbsp sauce flour

100ml skimmed milk

salt and black pepper

1 dsp wholegrain Dijon mustard

1 dsp smooth Dijon mustard (see Tip)

1 tbsp chopped fresh parsley, to garnish

1 Heat half the oil in a large non-stick frying pan, then add the chicken and cook over a high heat, turning occasionally, until golden all over. Remove with a slotted spoon and transfer to a casserole dish.

2 Add the shallots and half the remaining oil and a tablespoon or so of stock if the mix becomes too dry, stir for a few minutes over a medium-high heat until they are tinged brown, then transfer them to the casserole with a slotted spoon.

3 Arrange the carrots and leeks in the casserole dish with the chicken and shallots.

4 Reduce the heat to medium, add the rest of the oil and the flour to the pan and stir for a minute, then gradually add the stock, stirring all the time, until you have a sauce.

5 Add the milk and seasoning and combine well, then pour the sauce over the chicken and vegetables, cover the casserole dish and cook in a preheated oven, 170°C/335°F/Gas 3½, for 45 minutes or until everything is tender and the chicken is cooked through (see Tip).

6 Stir the two mustards into the sauce thoroughly, and serve garnished with the parsley.

serving suggestion Serve with boiled potatoes and green beans or broccoli.

tips I use two types of mustard because the wholegrain mustard gives an interesting visual appeal to the dish, while the smooth one adds to the creamy texture, but you don't have to use both if you don't want to – 1 tablespoon of either will be fine.

If you happen to make this dish in the summer, add some asparagus tips for the last few minutes of cooking; they make it luxurious and even tastier. Artichoke hearts from a jar (well drained) are another good addition towards the end of cooking.

coq au vin

The classic French dish is high in calories and quite time-consuming to make – this version keeps the taste without the fat and is also quick to prepare.

Serves 4 | 425 calories per portion | 17g fat per portion

1 tbsp olive oil

15g butter

100g lean smoked back bacon, cut into strips

2 medium onions, thinly sliced (see Tip)

8 skinless chicken thighs (800g total weight)

2 cloves garlic, crushed

1 tbsp seasoned flour (see Tip)

2 tbsp brandy

200g mushrooms, sliced (see Tip)

½ bottle of French red wine

150ml strong chicken stock

2 tbsp chopped fresh parsley

few sprigs of fresh thyme or 1 tsp dried thyme

1 bay leaf

salt and black pepper

1 Heat half the oil with the butter in a large, lidded non-stick frying pan or flameproof casserole and cook the bacon and onions for a few minutes over a medium-high heat until the onions have softened. Remove with a slotted spoon and reserve.

2 Add the chicken to the pan in two batches with the remaining oil and brown over a high heat on all sides, then return the onion and bacon to the pan with the garlic, flour and brandy, and stir for 1–2 minutes.

3 Add the mushrooms, wine, stock, herbs and seasoning, stir well and bring to the boil. Reduce the heat, cover and simmer gently for 45 minutes or until the chicken is cooked through.

4 Transfer the chicken and vegetables to a warm serving dish using a slotted spoon and keep warm while you increase the heat and cook the sauce for a few minutes until reduced, thickened and rich.

5 Check the seasoning and remove the bay leaf, then pour the sauce over the chicken.

serving suggestion Mashed potatoes and Savoy cabbage or steamed courgettes are good with this dish.

tips You can use 12 shallots instead of the onions, which would look more attractive for a dinner party and the flavour will be a little sweeter.

Seasoned flour is simply plain flour with the addition of salt and black pepper.

For this recipe it is best to choose small chestnut-type mushrooms, which won't discolour the sauce.

casseroles, braises and stews

cheat's cassoulet

Cassoulet is a warming winter supper. In this version, the fat content has been reduced to just 25 per cent of the classic recipe, but the taste is all still there.

Serves 4 | 425 calories per portion | 17.5g fat per portion

1½ tbsp olive oil

4 large skinless, bone-in chicken thighs (400g total weight)

4 extra-lean large pork sausages or venison sausages, halved

100g lean smoked back bacon, chopped

1 large Spanish onion, finely chopped

3 cloves garlic, crushed

100ml dry white wine

100ml chicken stock

400g can chopped tomatoes

400g can cannellini beans, drained and rinsed

1 bouquet garni

1 dsp tomato purée

salt and black pepper

50g coarse breadcrumbs (see Tip)

1 tbsp chopped fresh parsley

1 Heat half the oil in a lidded non-stick frying pan with a heatproof handle or a flameproof casserole, and cook the chicken and sausage pieces over a high heat until browned on all sides, adding the bacon for the last minute or two. Remove with a slotted spoon and reserve.

2 Add the rest of the oil and the onion and sauté over a medium heat for about 10 minutes until softened. Stir in the rest of the ingredients, except the breadcrumbs and parsley, and season. Bring to the boil, then reduce the heat, cover and simmer gently for 30 minutes.

3 Remove the lid, stir and cook for another 20 minutes or until the chicken is cooked through.

4 Preheat the grill to medium. Remove the bouquet garni from the casserole and check the seasoning, adjusting to taste.

5 Mix the breadcrumbs with the parsley and sprinkle the mixture over the top of the cassoulet, then brown under the grill and serve.

serving suggestion Serve with boiled potatoes and green beans.

tip For coarse breadcrumbs, use slightly stale bread and crumble it between your fingers, rather than using a processor. Otherwise, cut the bread into tiny cubes using a bread knife.

pheasant breasts in red wine

Pheasants can be bought from October to the end of January and are a very flavoursome alternative to chicken. Although they have a higher fat content, a little goes a long way, since they are quite rich.

Serves 4 | 400 calories per portion | 18g fat per portion

1 tbsp olive oil
4 pheasant breasts
(560g total weight)
2 rashers lean back bacon, chopped
2 small or 1 large sticks celery, finely chopped
1 small onion, finely chopped
150ml chicken stock
150ml red wine
1 bay leaf
salt and pepper
2 tbsp half-fat crème fraîche

1 Heat half the oil in a flameproof casserole and cook the pheasant breasts and the bacon over a high heat until the pheasant is browned all over (see Tip). Transfer the breasts to a plate with a slotted spoon and set aside.

2 Sauté the celery and onion in the remaining oil for 5 minutes until softened, adding a little water or chicken stock if they look too dry.

3 Return the pheasant to the casserole; pour the stock and wine in, add the bay leaf and season with black pepper and a very little salt. Bring to a simmer, then cover and cook in a preheated oven, 170°C/335°F/Gas 3½, for about 40 minutes or until the breasts are cooked through.

4 Remove the breasts and keep warm. Put the casserole back on the hob. Bring to a fast boil and cook for about 5 minutes until the liquid has reduced by half (see Tip).

5 Remove from the heat, stir the crème fraîche and check for seasoning. Serve the breasts surrounded with the sauce.

serving suggestion Brussels sprouts, carrots and mashed potato are good accompaniments to the pheasant.

tips If you don't have a flameproof casserole, sauté the meat and vegetables in a non-stick frying pan, then add the liquids, bring everything to a simmer and transfer the contents of the pan to an ordinary casserole. Another alternative, using a flameproof casserole or a lidded non-stick frying pan, is to simmer the dish very gently on the hob for about 25 minutes.

Be patient about reducing the sauce – if you don't do this, it will be too thin and won't have as much flavour.

casseroles, braises and stews

winter game and mushroom casserole

Venison and rabbit make excellent low-fat casseroles without drying out or becoming tough. This one is excellent for a dinner party.

Serves 4 | 340 calories per portion | 11g fat per portion

1 tbsp olive oil

600g stewing venison, cubed (see Tip)

16 small shallots, peeled

2 green peppers, deseeded and cut into squares

2 cloves garlic, crushed

1 bay leaf

few sprigs of fresh thyme or 1 tsp dried thyme

6 juniper berries

1 tbsp plain flour

50ml brandy

200ml red wine

150ml beef stock

1 tbsp tomato purée

salt and black pepper

225g chestnut mushrooms, sliced

1 Heat half the oil in a good quality, lidded non-stick frying pan or flameproof casserole (see Tip) and cook the meat in two batches over a high heat until browned all over. Remove from the pan with a slotted spoon and reserve.

2 Add the shallots and peppers with the rest of the oil and cook for a few minutes until coloured a little, then add the garlic and stir for 1 minute.

3 Reduce the heat a little and return the meat to the pan with the bay leaf, thyme, juniper berries and flour. Stir well, then add the brandy, wine, stock and tomato purée with some seasoning and stir again. Bring to the boil, then reduce the heat, cover and simmer gently for 1 hour.

4 Add the mushrooms and cook for a further 30 minutes or until the meat and vegetables are tender. Check the seasoning and adjust to taste.

serving suggestion Potato and celeriac mash and white cabbage are perfect with the casserole.

tips You can use rabbit fillets instead of the venison or a mixture of the two meats – some butchers or supermarkets stock mixed game packs.

If you don't have a heavy-duty, lidded frying pan or a flameproof casserole, use an ordinary non-stick frying pan to brown the meat and vegetables, then transfer everything to a casserole dish and cook in a preheated oven, 170°C/335°F/Gas 3½, for the same length of time.

rabbit and cider casserole

Rabbit is a much underused meat – it is very low in fat, inexpensive and tastes delicious, like delicate chicken meat.

Serves 4 | 330 calories per portion | 12.5g fat per portion

8 good meaty rabbit joints, (about 800–900g total weight), on the bone (see Tip)

1 large onion, chopped

1 large cooking apple, peeled, cored and cut into about 12 wedges

80g ready-to-eat stoned prunes, halved

100g lean gammon, chopped

salt and black pepper

1 tsp dried sage

½ tsp ground nutmeg

200ml chicken stock

200ml dry cider

15g butter

1 tbsp plain flour

1 Put the rabbit pieces in a family-sized flameproof casserole dish and scatter the onion around. Arrange the apple wedges, prunes and gammon between the joints, season well and sprinkle over the sage and nutmeg.

2 Heat the chicken stock and cider to just below boiling point and pour them over the casserole, cover and simmer gently for 1¼ hours or until the rabbit and onion are cooked through (see Tip).

3 Spoon off about 75ml (5 tablespoons) of the casserole gravy into a jug and put the lid back on.

4 Heat the butter in a small non-stick saucepan and stir in the flour over a medium heat. Add a little of the casserole gravy and mix with a wooden spoon over the heat, adding a little more gravy until you have used all of it.

5 Return the gravy to the casserole dish and stir well, bring back to a simmer and cook, covered, for a further 10 minutes. Check the seasoning and serve.

serving suggestion Serve with boiled potatoes and spring greens.

tips Discard the rib joints as they don't contain enough meat to warrant cooking them. If the rabbit is small, you may need three jointed pieces per person.

You can cook the casserole in a preheated oven, 170°C/335°F/Gas 3½ for 1¼ hours.

casseroles, braises and stews

bouillabaisse

For people who find fish boring, this is a magnificent recipe, full of colour, aroma and flavour. It would be a good supper party dish.

Serves 4 | 370 calories per portion | 10.5g fat per portion

1½ tbsp olive oil

1 large onion (about 200g), finely chopped

1 medium leek, finely chopped

2 cloves garlic, crushed

400g can peeled plum tomatoes

1 tsp fennel seed

1 bay leaf

1 sachet of saffron threads in 1 tbsp hot water

2 strips orange zest

850ml fish stock (see Tip)

salt and black pepper

450g white mixed fish fillets, cut into large chunks (see Tip)

400g mullet, bass or bream fillet (see Tip)

225g mussels in shell, cleaned and prepared (see Tip)

225g prawns or squid or scallops (see Tip)

1 tbsp chopped fresh parsley, to garnish

1 Heat the oil in a good quality, lidded non-stick frying pan or flameproof casserole and sauté the onion and leek over a medium-high heat until softened and just turning golden. Add the garlic and stir for 1 minute.

2 Add the tomatoes, herbs, saffron, orange zest, stock and seasoning, stir well and bring to a simmer. Cook, covered, for 5 minutes.

3 Add all the fish and seafood, bring back to a simmer and cook for another 5 minutes with the lid on, or until all the mussel shells have opened (discard any that don't open).

4 Check for seasoning and remove the orange peel, then, using a slotted spoon, arrange the fish and shellfish in serving bowls, distributing the different types evenly. Pour plenty of the sauce over and serve garnished with the parsley.

serving suggestion Crusty French or Italian bread, followed by a salad are all you need with the fish stew.

tips Ask your fishmonger for all the bones and surplus bits after the fish have been filleted, then use them to make your own Fish Stock (see page 222). Otherwise, use fresh chilled fish stock from the supermarket.

For the white fish fillet, try to get the tastier, meatier varieties of fish, such as monkfish or swordfish. Haddock and even cod tend to break up too easily.

Small whole fish, such as red mullet or sea bass, make this dish special, so do try to include them.

Mussels in the shell look more attractive than the shelled mussels. However, if you do use shelled mussels, reduce the weight to 150g.

Try to use fresh prawns, squid or scallops as they will make the finished dish much tastier.

moroccan spiced fish tagine

Serves 4 | 330 calories per portion | 16g fat per portion

4 cod fillets, (about 200g each)
1 quantity Chermoula (see page 64),
omitting the onion
½ preserved lemon
1 medium carrot, very thinly
sliced lengthways
1 medium courgette, very thinly
sliced lengthways
200g can peeled plum
tomatoes, halved
200ml fish stock (see Tip, page 90)
8 black stoned olives, halved
salt and black pepper

1 Rub the fillets with the chermoula, place them in a shallow dish with the preserved lemon scattered around and leave to marinate in the fridge for 2 hours, spooning the marinade over the fish occasionally.

2 Put the carrot and courgette in the base of a shallow flameproof casserole with the tomatoes, place the fish on top, then spoon over the marinade and pour the stock around the edges of the dish.

3 Scatter the olives on top, season well and bring to a simmer on the hob. Simmer very gently for 20 minutes or until the fish is opaque but still moist, or cook in a preheated oven, 170°C/335°F/Gas 3½, for 30 minutes.

4 Using a fish slice, serve everyone a fillet each on its own bed of vegetables with 2–3 spoonfuls of the casserole liquid.

ⓥ sweet potato and spinach curry

Serves 4 | 205 calories per portion | 5g fat per portion

1 tbsp olive oil
1 large onion, finely chopped
1 clove garlic, crushed
1 tbsp Dry Spice Mix (see page 221)
2 large or 4 small sweet potatoes
(600g total weight), peeled and
cut into bite-sized cubes
(see Tip)
250ml vegetable stock
1 large tomato, roughly chopped
salt and black pepper
300g pack ready-washed leaf
spinach, tough stalks removed
and leaves torn

1 Heat the oil in a lidded non-stick frying pan or flameproof casserole and sauté the onion over a medium-high heat, stirring frequently, until softened and just turning golden. Add the garlic and dry spice mix and stir for 1 minute.

2 Add the potatoes, stock, tomato and seasoning, and bring to the boil. Reduce the heat, cover and simmer over a low heat, stirring occasionally, for 30 minutes or until the potatoes are tender.

3 Rinse the spinach in cold running water and, with the water still clinging to the leaves, cook in a saucepan over a medium-high heat for 1 minute, stirring, until wilted.

4 Stir the spinach into the curry and cook for a few minutes without the lid, stirring from time to time. By the time the curry is ready, it should be quite dry, as most of the stock should have evaporated.

serving suggestion This curry is delicious with a lentil dhal, rice, mango chutney and low-fat natural bio yogurt.

tip You need to use the orange-fleshed sweet potatoes, not the white-fleshed yams – scrape back a little of the skin with a fingernail to make sure you have the right sort. The taste of the orange ones is much sweeter and the texture finer.

italian bean stew

Serves 4 | 250 calories per portion | 4.5g fat per portion

1 tbsp olive oil
1 large onion, chopped
2 medium sticks celery, chopped
1 large carrot, sliced into rounds
2 cloves garlic, crushed
400g can borlotti beans, drained and rinsed (see Tip)
300ml passata
1 tsp chopped fresh rosemary
300ml vegetable stock (see Tip)
1 tsp sugar
salt and black pepper
125g pasta shapes (see Tip)
1 tbsp chopped fresh parsley, to garnish

1 Heat the oil in a lidded non-stick frying pan or flameproof casserole and sauté the onion, celery and carrot over a medium-high heat for 5 minutes until softened. Add the garlic and stir for 1 minute.

2 Add the beans, passata, rosemary, stock, sugar and seasoning, and simmer, covered, for 30 minutes.

3 Add the pasta and simmer for another 15 minutes, then check the seasoning. If the stew seems a bit dry, add a little water or vegetable stock, stir and reheat.

4 Serve garnished with the parsley.

serving suggestion This is a complete meal, but you could add some crusty bread and a green salad.

tips Use cannellini beans or butter beans instead of the borlotti beans.
    Use good quality vegetable bouillon, such as Marigold, or use the Basic Vegetable Stock recipe on page 222.
    For a change, use wholewheat pasta shapes and cook for an extra 5 minutes or until tender.

casseroles, braises and stews

93

ⓥ caponata

This is a delicious rich aubergine stew from Italy. The original version is a side dish but by adding protein in the form of lentils, you have a more substantial and satisfying main meal.

Serves 4 | 240 calories per portion | 10g fat per portion

125g dried brown lentils

2 large aubergines (500g total weight), cut into 1.5cm thick diagonal slices

2 tbsp olive oil

2 large onions, thinly sliced

2 sticks celery, chopped

400g can plum tomatoes (see Tip)

12 green stoned olives, rinsed and halved

1 dsp capers, rinsed and drained

1 dsp sugar

1 tbsp balsamic vinegar

1 tbsp red wine vinegar

salt and black pepper

1–2 tbsp water

1 tbsp pinenuts, to serve

1 Cover the lentils with water in a saucepan and cook for 30 minutes until tender; drain and reserve.

2 Brush the aubergines with half the oil. Bake in a preheated oven, 180°C/350°F/Gas 4, for 20 minutes until golden and just softened.

3 Meanwhile, heat the rest of the oil in a lidded non-stick frying pan and sauté the onions and celery over a medium-high heat until softened, then add the tomatoes, olives, capers, sugar, vinegars, seasoning and lentils to the pan with the aubergine slices and water, stir well and bring to the boil.

4 Reduce the heat, cover and simmer over a very low heat for 30 minutes or until everything is tender, adding a drop or two of water during this time if it looks too dry.

5 Meanwhile, toast the pinenuts in a small non-stick frying pan over a high heat for a few minutes until golden (watch them for as soon as they begin to change colour, they will burn very quickly).

6 Check the seasoning and scatter the pinenuts over the caponata before serving.

serving suggestion Serve simply with crusty Italian bread or pasta and a green salad.

tip If tomatoes are in season and you can find some really tasty ripe fresh ones, use 4–5 instead of the canned ones, chopping them roughly.

ⓥ vegetable chilli

This chilli is so hearty that nobody will notice there is no meat in it.

Serves 4 | 230 calories per portion | 4.5g fat per portion

1 tbsp groundnut oil

2 medium red onions, thinly sliced

1 red and 1 yellow pepper
deseeded and chopped

2 cloves garlic, crushed

2 bird's eye chillies (see Tip)

1 tsp each ground coriander
and cumin seeds

1 tsp ground chilli powder (see Tip)

1 small butternut squash, peeled,
deseeded and cut into
bite-sized cubes

400g new potatoes, well scrubbed
and cut into bite-sized cubes

2 medium courgettes, sliced

400g can chopped tomatoes

100g black-eyed beans (cooked
weight, see Tip)

1 tbsp tomato purée

200ml vegetable stock

salt and black pepper

Tabasco, to taste

handful of fresh coriander,
to garnish

1 Heat the oil in a large, lidded non-stick frying pan (see Tip) and sauté the onions and peppers over a medium-high heat for 5 minutes until softened and just turning golden. Add the garlic, chillies, coriander, cumin and chilli powder, and stir for 1–2 minutes.

2 Add the remaining ingredients, except the Tabasco and coriander, stir well and bring to the boil.

3 Reduce the heat, cover and simmer gently for 45 minutes or until all the vegetables are tender. Halfway through the cooking time, test the sauce for heat and add a little Tabasco, if you like.

4 Check the seasoning and serve the chilli garnished with fresh coriander.

serving suggestion Serve with rice and drizzle the curry with low-fat natural bio yogurt or with half-fat Greek yogurt, which is slightly higher in fat and calories.

tips Bird's eye chillies are quite hot, but if you like a hot curry add more to taste. You can also add more or less chilli powder.

A 400g can of black-eyed beans will provide a surplus of 150g beans – these can be frozen or mashed with olive oil and lemon juice and used as a dip.

You will need quite a large and wide lidded frying pan (or flameproof casserole) to cook this chilli – if you don't have one big enough, use a standard frying pan and after you have sautéed the onion, peppers and spices, transfer them to a large lidded saucepan with the rest of the ingredients and continue the recipe. Alternatively, transfer them to an ovenproof casserole dish and cook in a preheated oven, 180°C/350°F/Gas 4, for 1 hour or until all the vegetables are tender.

95

casseroles, braises and stews

roasts and bakes

Roasting and baking are two great ways to cook meat, poultry, game and fish with little need for extra fat. However, plain roasting of low-fat cuts can give a dry and disappointing result. The recipes in this chapter add moisture as well as flavour, colour and texture, so that the finished result is always succulent.

Much of the advice previously given for grilling is appropriate for roasting – if you have time to first marinate your meat or fish, or create a crust or paste for it, the finished dish will be much more rewarding.

Low-fat oven cooking can also mean cooking 'en papillote' – wrapping the food with flavourings in a foil or parchment parcel. When you open the parcel, the aromas are stunning!

I have also used the oven to cook what many people regard as traditional fried foods, such as fish and chips, and Southern 'fried' chicken. These dishes retain all the flavour and appearance without the fat.

This chapter includes several delicious pies and tray bakes; these are personal favourites of mine and frequently consumed with gusto in our household.

Most of the recipes include tips and variations so that you need never serve up a 'boring' roast again.

roast beef with red wine gravy

Roast beef shouldn't be off the menu even if you're watching the fat – lean beef is, actually, a low-fat food. Rib and sirloin roasts contain much more fat, while topside is a very lean cut, so it can tend to dryness. Use this method to keep it succulent.

Serves 4–6 | For 6: 265 calories per portion | 7.5g fat per portion
For 4: 400 calories per portion | 11g fat per portion

1 tbsp dry mustard powder
1 tbsp plain flour
1 heaped tsp dried or 2 tsp fresh thyme leaves
salt and black pepper
900g joint topside of beef
1 large onion, cut into 1cm thick horizontal slices
2 tbsp water

FOR THE GRAVY
10g plain flour
150ml red wine
150ml beef stock

1 Mix together the mustard, flour, thyme and seasoning in a bowl, then spread the mixture all over the beef joint, pressing it in well.

2 Arrange the slices of onion in the centre of a good quality heavy roasting tin to form a solid base, and sit the beef on top of the onion.

3 Add the water to the tin and roast the beef in a preheated oven, 180°C/350°F/Gas 4, for 1 hour or longer if you like your meat well done, basting once or twice with any juices from the pan. Add a little red wine and/or water if the tin becomes dry. Remove the meat from the roasting tin to a carving dish, cover with foil and leave to rest in a warm place for 10 minutes. (Leave the onion pieces in the pan.)

4 Tip the pan so that the juices run to a corner, spoon off most of the fat that appears and discard, leaving a small amount of meaty juices and sediment. Heat the pan on the hob and add the flour to the pan, stirring well with a wooden spoon for 1–2 minutes.

5 Add the wine and stock, and bring to a rolling boil, stirring, for a few minutes until you have a gravy the consistency of single cream. Pour the juices that have run from the meat into the gravy. Pour the gravy through a sieve and into a warm jug.

6 Carve the meat into thin slices and serve with the gravy.

serving suggestion Serve the beef with unpeeled baby new potatoes, brushed with olive oil, seasoned and roasted in another pan, plus a selection of fresh vegetables and some horseradish sauce (see Tip).

tip To make horseradish sauce, mix 1 dessertspoon grated horseradish root (available in jars) with 2 tablespoons half-fat crème fraîche.

roasts and bakes

cottage pie

Cottage pie is surely the all-time traditional British family favourite supper, and it is easy to see why. This version is probably even better than the original.

Serves 4 | 400 calories per portion | 16g fat per portion

1 tbsp groundnut oil
400g extra lean beef, minced
1 large onion (about 200g), finely chopped
1 stick celery, finely chopped
1 large carrot (about 150g), peeled and finely chopped
200g can baked beans in tomato sauce
1 tbsp tomato purée
1 dsp mixed dried herbs
1 tsp Worcestershire sauce
salt and black pepper
300ml beef stock

FOR THE TOPPING
300g old potatoes, peeled and cubed
200g parsnips, cubed (see Tip)
1 tbsp light mayonnaise
2 tbsp low-fat natural fromage frais
skimmed milk, if necessary
1 tbsp grated Parmesan cheese

1 Heat half the oil in a large non-stick frying pan and sauté the beef for a few minutes, stirring occasionally, until browned. Transfer it to a bowl with a slotted spoon, tilting the pan so that any melted fat and oil are left behind, and discard.

2 Add the onion, celery, carrot and the rest of the oil to the pan and sauté over a medium heat for about 10 minutes or until softened, adding a little water if it looks too dry.

3 Return the meat to the pan and mix in well. Roughly mash the baked beans with their tomato sauce – not too finely – and add them to the pan with the tomato purée, herbs, Worcestershire sauce, black pepper and stock.

4 Stir everything very well, then bring to the boil. Reduce the heat, cover and simmer for about 45 minutes, stirring once or twice and adding a little water or stock, if you think it looks too dry.

5 Meanwhile, make the topping. Boil the potatoes and parsnips together in salted water until tender; drain, leaving about 1 tablespoon of the cooking water in the pan. Mash them with the mayonnaise, fromage frais, then season to taste and mash again. If the mixture seems too dry, add a little skimmed milk to get the right consistency.

6 When the meat mixture is cooked, check it for seasoning and add a little salt if necessary, then spoon evenly into a family-sized pie dish and smooth the vegetable purée over the top.

7 Top with the cheese and bake in a preheated oven, 180°C/350°F/ Gas 4, for 25 minutes or until golden.

serving suggestion Steamed spring greens or broccoli and perhaps some petit pois are all you need with this pie.

tip If the parsnips are old, you may need to remove the core; quarter the parsnips lengthways and cut out the darker central section.

shepherd's rosti lamb pie

Lamb is never going to be extremely low in fat as it is naturally one of the fattier meats you can buy. However, this recipe brings the fat and calorie levels down very nicely without losing flavour. Remember to do the first stage of cooking the day before you want to eat the pie.

Serves 4 | 400 calories per portion | 20g fat per serving

450g lean lamb mince (see Tip)

1 medium onion (about 150g), finely chopped

1 large clove garlic, finely chopped

1 tbsp chopped fresh mint

1 tsp each of dried oregano and rosemary

10g sun-dried tomato paste from a jar

250ml ready-made traditional Italian tomato sauce from a jar

stock

salt and black pepper

FOR THE TOPPING

500g old potatoes, peeled and cubed

½ tbsp olive oil

50g feta cheese, finely crumbled

1   Put the lamb in a good quality, heavy non-stick frying pan and heat slowly so that it begins to cook in its own fat. Increase the heat to high, cook, stirring from time to time, until the lamb is lightly browned.

2   Push the lamb to the edges of the pan and add the onion to the centre. Reduce the heat a little and sauté the onion for about 10 minutes, adding the garlic for the last 3 minutes of cooking and a little water if necessary. Mix well, remove from the heat, cover with foil and allow the mixture to cool, then place in the fridge overnight.

3   Take the pan out of the fridge and, using clean fingers or a spoon, remove any solidified fat that you can see on the top and sides of the pan. Return the pan to the hob and warm over a medium heat, adding the herbs, tomato paste and tomato sauce. If the mixture looks too solid when it is warm, add a little stock and stir in well.

4   Cover and simmer for 30 minutes, then check the seasoning, adding salt and pepper to taste.

5   Meanwhile, parboil the potatoes in lightly salted water until almost cooked through; drain well and allow to cool a little. Grate coarsely into a mixing bowl, then combine with the oil and feta cheese; season to taste.

6   When the lamb mixture is cooked, spoon it into a family-sized pie dish, smooth down the top and cover with the potato mixture. Bake in a preheated oven, 180°C/350°F/Gas 4, for 30 minutes or until the top is golden.

serving suggestion Serve the pie with green beans or any plainly cooked green vegetable.

tip Check the lamb contains no more than 10g fat per 100g meat.

roasts and bakes

moussaka

This recipe for the Greek favourite reduces the fat in the traditional recipe by two-thirds – though it is still higher than many main courses in this book! However, it's well within bounds for an average low-fat maintenance diet, so enjoy.

Serves 4 | 420 calories per portion | 23.5g fat per portion

2 medium aubergines, sliced into 1cm rounds
½ tbsp olive oil
salt and black pepper
350g lean lamb, minced
1 large onion, finely chopped
1 clove garlic, finely chopped
1 tsp dried oregano
1 tsp ground cinnamon
1 tbsp tomato purée
150ml beef stock (see Tip)

FOR THE TOPPING
400ml skimmed milk
30g sauce flour (see Tip)
1 tsp dry mustard
80g Gruyère cheese, grated (see Tip)
1 medium egg, beaten (see Tip)
25g fresh white breadcrumbs

1 Brush the aubergines with the oil and season. Place on a baking tray and roast in a preheated oven, 180°C/350°F/Gas 4, for about 20 minutes until softened and just turning golden; set aside.

2 Put the lamb into a good quality non-stick frying pan and heat gently for 5 minutes, so that the fat begins to run out and the meat cooks in its own fat, stirring from time to time. Add the onion and garlic and cook over a medium heat, stirring again, for a further 10 minutes.

3 Add the oregano, cinnamon, tomato purée and stock, and bring to the boil. Reduce the heat, cover and simmer over a medium heat for 30 minutes.

4 Meanwhile, make the topping sauce. Pour the milk into a non-stick saucepan, add the flour, mustard and seasoning and whisk constantly over a medium heat until the milk begins to simmer and the sauce thickens. Add two-thirds of the grated cheese and stir until it melts. Take off the heat, check the seasoning, add the beaten egg, stir well to combine and set aside.

5 When the lamb mixture is cooked, spoon it into a family-sized pie dish, top with the aubergine slices to cover the meat completely, and pour the sauce over the top. Combine the breadcrumbs with the remaining grated cheese and sprinkle it over the top of the aubergines. Increase the heat to 190°C/375°F/Gas 5, and bake for 25 minutes or until the top is golden.

serving suggestion Serve with a green salad.

tips Swap half the stock for red wine, for few extra calories and no more fat.
You can buy sauce flour in 450g packets in most supermarkets – it is so fine you don't need to add fat to make a smooth béchamel-type sauce.
If you swap the Gruyère cheese for half-fat Cheddar this will save you 30 calories and nearly 4g fat per portion, but it won't be as tasty.
Don't omit the egg – it makes the topping authentically 'wobbly firm'.

chinese oven-barbecued pork with stir-fried vegetables

Pork fillet is a great meat for fat-watchers as it is so lean – this recipe adds a little 'healthy' oil and bags of flavour.

Serves 4 | 265 calories per portion | 10g fat per portion

450g pork fillet (tenderloin), cut into 1cm slices

60ml hoisin sauce (see Tip)

30ml soy sauce

2 tbsp runny honey

2 tbsp sake or dry sherry

1 tsp Chinese five spice

1 tsp wholegrain mustard

1 tbsp groundnut oil

FOR THE STIR-FRIED VEGETABLES

½ tbsp sesame oil

8 medium spring onions, halved lengthways

1 medium carrot, cut into julienne strips

100g fresh beansprouts

1 small leek, cut into thin 5cm strips

50g mangetout or fine beans

1 Arrange the pork in a single layer in the base of a shallow, non-metallic dish.

2 Mix together the next seven ingredients in a small bowl, then pour the mixture over the pork and make sure everything is thoroughly coated. Leave, covered, in the fridge to marinate for a few hours or overnight.

3 Put the pork and some of the marinade in a small roasting pan (see Tip) and roast in a preheated oven, 180°C/350°F/Gas 4, for 25 minutes, basting once or twice.

4 Towards the end of the cooking time, heat a wok or non-stick frying pan with the sesame oil and stir-fry the vegetables for 3 minutes, adding 1 tablespoon of the pork marinade for the last minute of cooking time. Serve the pork with the vegetables.

serving suggestion Serve with plain boiled white rice or white rice noodles.

tips Hoisin sauce is widely available in jars at supermarkets.
   Make sure that the roasting pan isn't too large for the amount of pork, otherwise the juices will dry out.

roasts and bakes

moroccan stuffed roast lamb

This lamb is flavoured with a simple but gutsy spice paste based on the Moroccan 'ras el hanout'. It makes a great change from a plain roast.

Serves 6 | 375 calories per portion | 16.5g fat per portion (see Tip)

1 medium onion, chopped
2 cloves garlic, chopped
2 tsp each ground cumin and coriander seeds
1 tsp ground paprika
1 fresh red chilli, deseeded and chopped
½ tsp each ground ginger and nutmeg (see Tip)
1 tablespoon fresh chopped mint
salt and black pepper
2kg leg of lamb
glass of dry white wine

1. Blend all the ingredients, except the lamb and wine, together in an electric blender or grind them well with a pestle and mortar (see Tip). Season the spice paste.

2. Make slits in the lamb in several places, to a depth and width of about 1.5cm, and fill them with the spice paste.

3. Put the meat in a roasting tin with a little water and half the wine in the base and roast in a preheated oven, 200°C/400°F/Gas 6, for 30 minutes.

4. Reduce the heat to 180°C/350°F/Gas 4 and roast for a further 1 hour or longer or shorter, depending on how rare or well done you like your lamb.

5. When cooked to your liking, remove the roast to a carving dish and allow to rest for 10 minutes before carving. Meanwhile, spoon off most of the fat from the pan and add the remaining white wine and allow to bubble to make a 'jus' or gravy, then pour through a sieve to clear, if you like, before serving with the lamb.

serving suggestion Couscous or roast new potatoes and a salad are good with the roast lamb.

tips The calorie and fat counts are based on a 175g portion of lamb, the equivalent of about 4 slices.

Use ready-crushed ginger, which can be bought in small jars, to save time. Ground ginger isn't all that great in savoury spicy dishes; it's better to use fresh or that available in jars.

If using a pestle and mortar to make the paste, chop the onion very finely and crush the garlic well before adding them to the mortar.

chicken, bacon and mushroom parcels

This easy but impressive supper is perfect if friends come round to eat – take the parcels to the table.

Serves 4 | 230 calories per portion | 9g fat per portion

juice of 1 lemon

100ml (1 small glass) dry white wine

1 tbsp finely chopped fresh flat-leaf parsley, plus extra to garnish

½ tbsp finely chopped fresh thyme (or 1 tsp dried)

salt and black pepper

200g small chestnut mushrooms, thinly sliced (see Tip)

2 cloves garlic, crushed

15g butter, softened

4 skinless, boneless chicken breasts (about 125g each)

4 rashers extra-lean back bacon (about 100g total weight), cut into thin strips

cooking oil spray (see Tip)

1 Mix together the lemon juice, wine, herbs and seasoning in a bowl, and stir well. Add the mushrooms and mix well.

2 Mash the garlic into the butter with a little seasoning.

3 Place each chicken breast in the centre of a piece of foil, which is large enough to wrap the meat loosely. Bring the foil up around the chicken to make a loose bowl shape, then divide the wine and mushroom mixture evenly between the parcels, spooning it over the top of the breasts.

4 Divide the garlic butter between the four parcels, putting a knob on top of each chicken portion, then seal securely but not too tightly, leaving an 'air gap'.

5 Bake the parcels in a preheated oven, 200°C/400°F/Gas 6, for 25–30 minutes or until everything is cooked through. Meanwhile, fry the bacon strips in a non-stick pan, sprayed with a little cooking oil until crisp.

6 To serve, put each parcel on a plate and open slightly. Divide the bacon between the parcels, sprinkling it over the top of the chicken. Serve immediately, garnished with extra parsley.

serving suggestion Serve the chicken parcels with baked or mashed potatoes and broccoli.

tips You can use any tasty mushrooms, but avoid those with very dark open gills, as they will turn the juices in the parcels an unappetising greyish-brown colour. The small button mushrooms are quite tasteless and best avoided.

Cooking oil spray is available in supermarkets, usually positioned near the bottles of oil; it contains only 1 calorie and 0.1g fat per spray, and is enough to prevent foods sticking during cooking.

roasts and bakes

baked chicken and sweet peppers with gremolata

This is a really simple supper, made even more delicious with the addition of a traditional Italian garnish.

Serves 4 | 260 calories per portion | 11g fat per portion

1 tbsp balsamic vinegar

2 tbsp olive oil

salt and black pepper

4 chicken breasts (about 500g total weight), halved

2 red peppers and 2 yellow peppers, deseeded and quartered

2 large red onions, quartered

8 cloves garlic, unpeeled (see Tip)

FOR THE GREMOLATA

zest of 1 large or 2 small lemons

1 large clove garlic, finely chopped

1 tbsp fresh parsley, very finely chopped

1 tbsp fresh mint, very finely chopped

2 tbsp white breadcrumbs

1 Mix together the vinegar, oil and seasoning in a shallow dish and marinate the chicken breasts in the mixture for 1–2 hours, if possible.

2 Put the peppers, onions and garlic in a suitably sized roasting pan (see Tip), and pour as much of the marinade from the chicken pieces as you can on to the vegetables, mixing well with your hands. Add a few good twists of salt and pepper (see Tip).

3 Roast the vegetables in a preheated oven, 190°C/375°F/Gas 5, for 25 minutes, turning once. Meanwhile, mix together the gremolata ingredients in a bowl.

4 Add the chicken pieces to the roasting pan, placing them between the vegetables and tucking them in well. Sprinkle the gremolata over the chicken (some of it will fall on the vegetables but that doesn't matter).

5 Return the pan to the oven for a further 20–25 minutes until everything is cooked – check the chicken with a sharp knife or skewer (if the juices run clear, it is cooked). Sprinkle on a little balsamic vinegar and seasoning, then serve.

serving suggestion Pasta shapes or couscous are good with the chicken and peppers.

tips Old, dry garlic cloves are unsuccessful when roasted in this way; try to get new season's plump and juicy garlic bulbs.

Use a pan of a suitable size so that the vegetables are quite crowded.

For a complete meal in the pan, add 400g peeled and cubed par-boiled potato to the vegetables, plus an extra ½ tablespoon of the marinade.

roasts and bakes

tandoori chicken

Serves 4 | 225 calories per portion | 7.5g fat per portion

juice of ½ lemon

1 medium onion, cut into chunks

3 cloves garlic, crushed

2.5cm piece of fresh ginger, chopped

1 tbsp turmeric

1 tsp paprika

2 red chillies, deseeded

1 tbsp garam masala

200ml low-fat natural bio yogurt

2 skinless, bone-in free-range chicken breasts (about 175g each), halved

4 large skinless, bone-in free-range chicken thighs (about 100g each)

1 lemon, cut into 4 wedges

1 Blend the first eight ingredients together in an electric blender, adding a little of the yogurt if the mixture is too thick to blend well.

2 Stir the rest of the yogurt in thoroughly to combine. Coat all the chicken pieces and arrange them in a roasting dish. If possible, cover and leave in a cool place to marinate for a few hours.

3 Arrange the chicken on a solid baking tray, and roast in a preheated oven, 200°C/400°F/Gas 6, uncovered, for 25–30 minutes or until the chicken is cooked through and the juices run clear (the breasts may cook more quickly than the thighs, in which case remove them and keep warm).

4 Serve the chicken with the lemon wedges.

serving suggestion Serve the chicken with a tomato, onion, cucumber and coriander salad, as well as chapatis or basmati rice.

pesto-stuffed chicken breasts

Serves 4 | 220 calories per portion | 10.5g fat per portion

4 skinless, boneless chicken breasts (about 500g total weight)

4 tbsp ricotta cheese (see Tip)

60ml good quality black olive pesto

cooking oil spray

1 tbsp chopped fresh parsley, to garnish

1 Flatten the chicken breasts between non-stick baking parchment using a rolling pin (bash the chicken with the long side, don't roll).

2 Mix together the ricotta and pesto in a small bowl and spoon a quarter of it over the centre of each chicken breast. Roll up the chicken breasts and secure each one with two cocktail sticks.

3 Spray cooking oil lightly over the base of a small baking dish and add the chicken breasts. Spray the tops of the breasts, then cover with a small pieces of foil – just cover the breasts, not the whole dish.

4   Bake in a small roasting dish just large enough to hold the breasts with little space to spare in a preheated oven, 190°C/375°F/Gas 5, for 20–25 minutes or until the breasts are cooked, and serve with pan juices and parsley to garnish.

serving suggestion Tricolour pasta shapes of choice and a tomato salad are good partners with the chicken.

tip Use 30g fresh breadcrumbs instead of the ricotta, saving 40 calories and 4g fat per portion.

southern-baked chicken drumsticks

Serves 4 | 405 calories per portion | 20g fat per portion

100g fresh white breadcrumbs
40g Gruyère cheese, grated (see Tip)
1 tbsp finely chopped fresh oregano, or 1 tsp dried
salt and black pepper
150g fromage frais, 8% fat
50ml half-fat (light) mayonnaise
1 clove garlic, crushed (see Tip, page 70)
1 dsp sun-dried tomato paste
1 tbsp Dijon mustard
8 skinless, bone-in chicken drumsticks (about 100g each)

1   In a shallow bowl, mix together the breadcrumbs, cheese, oregano and seasoning.

2   In another bowl, mix together the fromage frais, mayonnaise, garlic, tomato paste and mustard with a little more seasoning.

3   Pat the chicken drumsticks dry with kitchen paper, then coat each one first in the fromage frais mixture, then in the breadcrumb mixture, laying each one on a solid baking tray as you do so.

4   Bake in a preheated oven, 180°C/350°F/Gas 4, for 45 minutes or until the coating is golden and the chicken is cooked through – the juices should run clear when the chicken is pricked with a sharp knife or skewer.

5   Serve the chicken hot or cold.

serving suggestion Serve with Crisp Potato Skins (see page 30), plus a tomato salsa.

tips I like to use Gruyère cheese for cooking as it is tastier than many other hard cheeses; a little goes a long way, and it also melts well.

roast turkey breast with apricot stuffing

Turkey is a super-lean meat and full of flavour (if you buy good quality). This joint is filled with a delicious, light, meat-free stuffing.

Serves 6 | 345 calories per portion | 6g fat per portion

125g basmati rice
250ml water, salted
1 tsp saffron threads
1 tbsp groundnut oil
1 small onion or 3–4 shallots, very finely chopped
2cm piece of fresh ginger, grated
125g ready-to-eat, dried apricots, finely chopped
20g pinenuts
1 tbsp chopped fresh parsley
1 tbsp chopped fresh coriander
zest and juice of 1 orange
1.5kg turkey breast joint (see Tip)
salt and black pepper

1 Place the rice, water and saffron threads in a saucepan. Bring to the boil over a medium heat. Reduce the heat, cover and simmer for about 15 minutes until tender and the water has been absorbed. Tip the rice into a mixing bowl and set aside (since the water is absorbed, draining shouldn't be necessary).

2 Heat the oil in a non-stick frying pan and sauté the onion for several minutes until softened and transparent. Add the ginger and apricots and stir for 1 minute, then add the pinenuts and some seasoning. Stir well and tip this mixture into the rice.

3 Add the herbs, orange zest and half the juice to the rice mixture; stir again. Spoon the rice mixture into the cavity of the turkey joint, squeeze the rest of the orange juice over the breast skin and cover with a piece of foil.

4 Roast the joint in a preheated oven, 180°C/350°F/Gas 4, for 1 hour, then remove the foil. Reduce the heat to 170°C/335°F/Gas 3½, and cook for a further 20–30 minutes until the breast juices run clear when pierced with a sharp knife or skewer.

5 Leave the turkey to stand for 10 minutes in a warm place, covered with foil, and serve 175g turkey per portion.

serving suggestion A salad of green leaves and cucumber, mixed with a few segmented orange slices and walnut halves, goes particularly well with the turkey.

tips Buy a turkey breast joint that is still on the breastbone so that you can stuff the cavity – don't buy the prepared turkey breast joints which are completely filleted, or you won't be able to stuff it.

If you prefer a firmer stuffing, which can be made into rolls or balls and cooked separately, add a beaten egg to the rice mixture. This will add 12 calories and 1g of fat per portion.

For a stuffing with even more kick, add a whole jalapeño chilli, deseeded and very finely chopped, to the stuffing mixture before cooking.

fish and chips

In this recipe, both the fish and the chips are baked, so they are not oily and there are no fishy cooking odours but still plenty of flavour. If you choose the baked cherry tomatoes as an accompaniment, you have a complete meal cooked in the oven.

Serves 4 | 475 calories per portion | 8.5g fat per portion

4 old potatoes (about 200g each), cut into wedges lengthways

1 tbsp groundnut or olive oil

salt and black pepper

1 tbsp olive oil

1 medium onion, finely chopped

1 clove garlic, finely chopped

150g coarse fresh breadcrumbs

1 tsp dried oregano

1 tbsp chopped fresh parsley

grated zest of 1 lemon

2 tbsp seasoned plain flour

2 egg whites, lightly beaten

4 haddock fillets (about 175g each), skin on (see Tip)

1 lemon, cut into wedges, to serve

1 Toss the potatoes in the groundnut or olive oil and season well. Place them on a solid baking tray and cook in a preheated oven, 200°C/400°F/Gas 6, for 30 minutes or until golden and crisp on the outside and cooked all the way through (see Tip).

2 Meanwhile, heat the oil in a non-stick frying pan and sauté the onion for a few minutes until softened and just turning golden. Stir in the garlic and cook for 1 minute, then stir in the breadcrumbs, herbs and lemon zest.

3 Spoon the flour on to a flat plate and place the egg whites in a shallow bowl.

4 Dip each haddock fillet first in the flour, then the egg whites and finally the breadcrumb mixture (don't coat the skin/underside). As you do so, lay each fillet on a solid baking tray, then put in the oven with the potatoes for the last 15 minutes of cooking until the crusts are golden and the fish is cooked through. Serve with the lemon wedges.

serving suggestion Serve with peas or roast cherry tomatoes. Put 400g cherry tomatoes in a baking dish, sprinkle with a little olive oil and seasoning, and roast with the potato wedges.

tips Haddock is my favourite 'frying' fish but cod fillets are fine in this recipe too.

If you have time, parboil the potato wedges for 3–4 minutes, drain well and pat dry before tossing in the olive oil – this tends to make the flesh slightly softer, while giving a crisper outer coating.

baked cod with mediterranean topping

Mediterranean flavours work well for people following low-fat or low-calorie diets, as they are so full of punch and give plenty of tastebud satisfaction – second only to Asian food in that respect.

Serves 4 | 225 calories per portion | 3.5g fat per portion

1 tbsp olive oil
1 medium onion, finely chopped
2 red peppers, deseeded and cut into small chunks
2 cloves garlic, crushed
1 red chilli, deseeded and finely chopped (see Tip)
400g can chopped tomatoes
1 tbsp tomato purée
pinch of brown sugar
salt and pepper
4 cod fillets (about 175g each)
8 black stoned olives, halved
chopped fresh parsley or basil, to garnish

1 Heat the oil in a non-stick frying pan and sauté the onion and peppers until softened and just turning golden. Add the garlic and chilli, and sauté for another minute.

2 Add the tomatoes, tomato purée, sugar and seasoning. Sauté over a low to medium heat for 30 minutes, stirring from time to time, or until the mixture is rich and has a thick sauce consistency.

3 Pat the cod fillets dry and place, skin-side down, on a baking tray. Spoon the sauce on top of each fillet and scatter the olives on top. Bake in a preheated oven, 180°C/350°F/Gas 4, for 15 minutes or until the cod is cooked through but still moist inside. Serve garnished with the parsley or basil.

serving suggestion New potatoes and green beans are ideal partners to the cod.

tip Omit the chilli, if preferred.

roasts and bakes

luxury fish pie

This lovely, creamy nursery food is also good enough to serve to friends.

Serves 4 | 505 calories per portion | 14.5g fat per portion

700g old potatoes, peeled and cubed

2 tbsp fromage frais, 8% fat

salt and black pepper

700ml semi-skimmed milk, infused (see Tip)

450g cod or haddock fillet

40g sauce flour

1 tsp mustard powder

80g Gruyère cheese, grated

juice of ½ lemon

100g small mushrooms, sliced

150g peeled prawns

1 large hard-boiled egg, roughly chopped

2 tbsp chopped fresh parsley

1 tbsp fresh breadcrumbs

1 tbsp grated Parmesan cheese

1 Boil the potatoes in salted water until tender, drain and mash with the fromage frais, seasoning and enough of the milk to make a nice smooth mash; set aside.

2 Put the fish in a non-stick frying pan and cover with the rest of the milk and some seasoning, and poach gently for a few minutes until just barely cooked. Remove the fish with a slotted spatula and transfer to a lipped chopping board, then pour the milk into a saucepan.

3 Flake the fish using your fingers and arrange the flakes evenly in the base of a family pie dish. Pour any juices on the board into the milk.

4 Add the flour and mustard powder to the milk and heat over a fairly gentle heat, whisking continuously, until you have a smooth sauce. Season well, and add the Gruyère and lemon juice.

5 Arrange the mushrooms, prawns and egg over the haddock and sprinkle with the parsley, then pour the sauce evenly over the dish.

6 Spoon or pipe the mashed potato around the inside edge of the dish and in a cross across the top of the pie. Mix together the breadcrumbs and Parmesan, sprinkle the mixture over the pie and bake in a preheated oven, 180°C/350°F/Gas 4, for 30 minutes or until golden.

serving suggestion Green beans and broccoli are good with the fish pie.

tip If you infuse the milk first, it will have a better flavour – put it in a pan on a very low heat with a few black peppercorns, a clove or two, a bay leaf and a small onion, halved. Don't let it boil – just keep it warm for an hour or so, then tip everything (including the seasonings) over the fish when you cook it. Remove the fish when cooked and pour the milk through a sieve, discarding the solids, before using it to make the white sauce.

salmon fishcakes

We should all try to eat oily fish once a week, and these fishcakes are an ideal way to get people who think they don't enjoy fish to love it. The saturated fat content is less than 4g a portion.

Serves 4 | 320 calories per portion | 16.5g fat per portion

400g old potatoes, peeled and cut into chunks (see Tip)

400g salmon fillet

2 tbsp half-fat mayonnaise

2 tbsp fromage frais, 8% fat

1 dsp basil pesto

1 green chilli, deseeded and very finely chopped

handful of fresh coriander

salt and black pepper

1 tbsp plain flour

½ tbsp olive oil

1 Cook the potatoes in boiling salted water until just tender. Meanwhile, place the salmon on a plate and microwave on medium-high for 4 minutes or poach gently in simmering water for a few minutes until just cooked (don't overcook or the cakes will be dry). Remove and discard the skin and flake the fish gently; reserve.

2 When the potatoes are cooked, drain and tip them into a large mixing bowl, then roughly mash so that you still have some small lumps left.

3 Stir the mayonnaise and fromage frais into the potato, then add the pesto, chilli, coriander and plenty of seasoning. Fold in the salmon, retaining whole flakes if you can.

4 Sprinkle the flour on to a chopping board, and make eight small cakes with the fish mixture, doing this as lightly as you can – you want a rustic look. Coat both sides of the cakes with the flour.

5 Brush both sides of the cakes with the oil, then, using a metal spatula, transfer them to a non-stick baking tray and bake in a preheated oven, 190°C/375°F/Gas 5, for 15 minutes or until lightly golden, turning carefully halfway through. Serve immediately.

serving suggestion Serve with a green salad and some Chilli Salsa (see page 30).

tip Use old, floury potatoes, such as King Edwards, to make the cakes.

roasts and bakes

roast monkfish with parma ham

This is a classic combination, though the herb content may vary. Monkfish is still an expensive fish, but it is worth splashing out for a dinner party.

Serves 4 | 235 calories per portion | 7.5g fat per portion

4 monkfish fillets (about 175g each; see Tip)

1 handful fresh basil leaves

1 tbsp olive oil

1 dsp sun-dried tomato paste

salt and black pepper

8 slices Parma ham (see Tip)

1 Make sure that the fish fillets have all the membrane removed and are clean and dry.

2 Using a pestle and mortar or a small electric blender, blend the basil with the oil, tomato paste and seasoning, adding a little water if necessary.

3 Coat the fish fillets with the paste (not over the ends) and leave to marinate for 1–2 hours, if possible.

4 Roll two slices of ham per fillet around the long sides of the fish and arrange each one in a smallish baking dish, side by side with the 'seam' at the bottom. Roast in a preheated oven, 190°C/375°F/Gas 5, for 20 minutes or until the fish is cooked through. Serve immediately.

serving suggestion Serve the monkfish with a green salad and some new potatoes or tabbouleh. It is also good with a fresh Tomato Sauce (see page 220).

tips You could, for a change, cut the monkfish into cubes before marinating. Thread them on to kebab sticks with the slices of ham in between, then grill.

Parma ham is very lean and has less than 30 calories a slice and only 1g fat.

potato parmigiana

Serves 4 | 250 calories per portion | 11g fat per portion

450g old potatoes, peeled and thickly sliced

1 large aubergine (about 300g), cut into 1cm thick slices

2 tbsp olive oil

salt and black pepper

1 medium onion, sliced

2 cloves garlic, crushed

400g can chopped tomatoes

1 heaped tbsp tomato purée

good handful of fresh basil

1 ball half-fat mozzarella cheese, thinly sliced

1 tbsp grated Parmesan cheese

green salad, to serve

1 Parboil the potatoes in salted water for about 6 minutes until just tender, then drain.

2 Meanwhile, toss the aubergine in half of the oil, season and arrange the slices on a solid tray. Roast in a preheated oven, 190°C/350°F/Gas 5, for 20 minutes or until golden and just tender.

3 While the potatoes and aubergines are cooking, heat the rest of the oil in a non-stick frying pan and sauté the onion until softened and just turning golden. Add the garlic and stir for a minute, then add the tomatoes, tomato purée, basil and seasoning; stir well.

4 Arrange half the aubergine slices in the base of a family-sized ovenproof dish, followed by half the tomato sauce, then half the potatoes. Repeat the layers and top with the mozzarella and Parmesan.

5 Bake in a preheated oven, 190°C/375°F/Gas 5, for 20 minutes or until the cheese has melted. Serve immediately with the salad.

tunisian eggs and peppers

Serves 2 | 245 calories per portion | 14.5g fat per portion

1 tbsp olive oil

4 mixed peppers, red, yellow and green (400g total weight), deseeded and thinly sliced

1 medium onion, sliced into rounds

1 tsp ground cumin

3 tomatoes, sliced (see Tip)

salt and black pepper

2 large free-range eggs

paprika, for sprinkling

1 Heat the oil in a non-stick frying pan and sauté the peppers and onion over a medium-high heat for 10 minutes, stirring frequently, until softened and just turning golden. Add the cumin and sauté for another minute.

2 Add the tomatoes and sauté for a few minutes more, then season and stir.

3 Transfer the pepper mixture to two individual gratin dishes and make a well in the centre.

4 Break an egg into each well and season again. Cover each dish with a small piece of foil and bake in a preheated oven, 190°C/375°F/ Gas 5, for 12 minutes or until the eggs are just set and the yolks are still runny. Serve sprinkled with paprika.

serving suggestion Crusty bread is good with the eggs.

tip Use canned tomatoes if you can't get really ripe and tasty fresh ones.

ⓥ summer vegetable gratin

Serves 4 | 260 calories per portion | 17g fat per portion

roasts and bakes

2 tbsp olive oil
2 red onions, sliced
2 yellow peppers, deseeded and sliced
2 medium courgettes, cut into 0.5cm thick slices
2 cloves garlic, crushed
1 small aubergine, cut into 0.5cm thick slices
250g fresh ripe tomatoes, halved or quartered, if large
250g chestnut mushrooms, sliced
75ml passata
salt and black pepper
1 large free-range egg, beaten
250g Greek yogurt
3 tbsp grated Parmesan cheese (about 30g)
pinch of ground nutmeg

1 Heat half the oil in a large non-stick frying pan or wok and sauté the onions, peppers and courgettes over a high heat, stirring constantly, until tender and turning golden.

2 Add the garlic and aubergine with the rest of the oil and stir-fry for a few more minutes, adding a little water if the mixture becomes too dry.

3 Add the tomatoes, mushrooms, passata and seasoning and stir-fry for a few minutes more over a medium heat, again adding a little water if necessary.

4 Tip the mixture into a family-sized baking dish and smooth the top.

5 Beat together the egg, yogurt, half the cheese, nutmeg and seasoning, and pour the mixture over the vegetables (see Tip). Sprinkle the rest of the Parmesan over the top.

6 Bake in a preheated oven, 190°C/375°F/Gas 5, for 30 minutes or until golden and bubbling. Serve immediately.

serving suggestion Serve with a large green salad and new potatoes.

tip This yogurt coating also makes a simple, relatively low-fat topping for Moussaka (see page 100).

[Ⓥ] winter root vegetable bake

This dish makes an easy one-pan supper for all the family.

Serves 4 | 320 calories per portion | 16.5g fat per portion

2 red onions, quartered

2 large carrots, cut into bite-sized chunks

2 parsnips, cut into bite-sized chunks

1 butternut squash, peeled, deseeded and cut into bite-sized chunks

250g potatoes, peeled and cut into bite-sized chunks

4–6 several cloves garlic, unpeeled

1½ tbsp olive oil

salt and black pepper

1 heaped tsp mixed dried herbs

100g ricotta cheese

200g Greek yogurt

1 free-range egg, beaten

2 tbsp grated Parmesan cheese (see Tip)

400g can chopped tomatoes

1 Put all the root vegetables and the garlic into a large roasting pan and toss well with the oil. Season well and sprinkle the herbs over the top. Bake in a preheated oven, 190°C/375°F/Gas 5, for 30 minutes, or until the vegetables are almost tender when pierced with a sharp knife, turning once.

2 Meanwhile, mix together the ricotta, yogurt, egg, Parmesan and some seasoning.

3 Remove the vegetables from the oven and pour the tomatoes over the top (they won't cover everything thoroughly but that doesn't matter). Reduce the heat to 180°C/350°F/Gas 4.

4 Pour the yogurt mixture over the top – again, it won't completely cover the vegetables. Return the pan to the oven and cook for a further 20 minutes or until the topping is set and golden and all the vegetables are tender.

serving suggestion This is a meal in itself but you could serve small portions of it with some lean roast beef or chicken.

tip Use Parmigiano Reggiano Parmesan cheese, not the ready-grated kind in tubs, which tends to be tasteless.

⊙ imam bayeldi

This is a Turkish dish translated as 'the priest fainted', so called, it is sometimes said, because he thought it tasted so delicious.

Serves 4 | 150 calories per portion | 7g fat per portion

2 large aubergines, halved (see Tip)
2 tbsp olive oil
1 medium onion, finely chopped
1 large green pepper, deseeded and finely chopped
1 clove garlic, crushed
50g raisins or sultanas
400g can tomatoes, roughly chopped (see Tip)
1 tsp soft dark brown sugar
1 tsp ground cinnamon
2 tbsp chopped fresh parsley
salt and pepper
100ml tomato juice

1 Scoop out most of the flesh from the aubergines (leaving a wall of flesh about 0.5–1cm thick still intact); chop the scooped-out flesh and retain.

2 Heat 1 tablespoon of the oil in a lidded non-stick frying pan and sauté the onion, pepper and garlic until softened and turning golden, then add the aubergine flesh, ½ tablespoon of oil and cook for a few more minutes.

3 Add the raisins or sultanas, tomatoes, sugar, cinnamon, half the parsley and plenty of seasoning, and cook, covered, for 30 minutes over a low heat, stirring occasionally and adding a little water or tomato juice if the mixture looks too dry.

4 Rub the remaining oil over the aubergine shells, inside and out, season and put them side by side in a baking dish with the remaining tomato juice, plus 1 tablespoon or so of water in the base.

5 Fill the aubergine cavities with the vegetable mixture and bake in a preheated oven, 190°C/375°F/Gas 5, for 40 minutes or until the aubergines have softened all the way through when pricked with a sharp knife or skewer. Sprinkle with the remaining parsley to serve.

serving suggestion Some couscous and a green herb salad are good with the aubergines. You can also use this dish as a starter or part of a buffet, in which case it would be nice to use the mini aubergines you can now buy.

tips It is sometimes recommended that aubergines are sprinkled with salt to remove any bitterness but I haven't done this for years and it doesn't seem to make any difference worth worrying about.
    You can use 3–4 large fresh tomatoes, roughly chopped, as long as they are tasty and ripe.

roasts and bakes

quick hob suppers

During the week, most people need a quick meal – something that is no hassle to put together and will be on the table in a matter of minutes.

All thirty recipes in this chapter fulfil these criteria – indeed, many take no more than 15–20 minutes from start to finish, and at most 30 minutes. All are cooked using minimal equipment, usually just one pan.

However, there the similarities end. You'll find a wide variety of tastes, flavours and ingredients in dishes made famous in all corners of the world, from Thai curries to Mediterranean dishes to Chinese stir-fries. There are ideas from Mexico, France, Spain, Africa and more.

A really good quality non-stick frying pan is the only real essential you may need to buy to make the following recipes – it will help to keep down the amount of fat you need to add to any dish and makes for more even and speedy cooking. You could also take some time to go through your storecupboard and stock up on ingredients that you'll call on time and time again for making quick, healthy meals, such as cooked pulses, cans of tomatoes, spices, herbs and seasonings.

Most of the quick hob suppers serve two but can easily be halved for lone diners and, if you have a really large pan, can be doubled to serve a family. You will find other ideas for quick suppers in the Grills (see page 50), Salads (page 176) and Pasta, Rice and Grains (page 150) chapters.

beef stroganoff

Possibly one of the most delicious quick suppers that you could rustle up. Although it is indulgent with ingredients, such as brandy and beef, it is still well within the boundaries of a low-fat main meal.

Serves 2 | 375 calories per portion | 18g fat per portion

1 tbsp olive oil
1 medium onion, finely chopped
300g lean rump steak, cut into thin strips
1 tsp Hungarian paprika (see Tip)
1 tsp sauce flour
200g small mushrooms, thinly sliced
1 tbsp brandy
50ml beef stock
salt and black pepper
100ml full-fat Greek yogurt
1 tbsp chopped fresh parsley, to garnish

1 Heat half the oil in a non-stick frying pan and sauté the onion over a medium-high heat for 10 minutes or until softened and just turning golden, then remove with a slotted spoon and reserve.

2 Add the rest of the oil to the pan, turn the heat up to full and sear the meat in two batches until browned on all sides – make sure the heat is high so that this will take only 1–2 minutes per batch.

3 Reduce the heat a little and return the first batch of meat and the onions plus all the juices to the pan, then add the paprika and flour and stir for 1–2 minutes.

4 Add the mushrooms, brandy, stock and seasoning, stir well, then bring to the boil. Reduce the heat and simmer gently on a low heat for 3 minutes, uncovered.

5 Stir in the Greek yogurt and warm through, then serve garnished with the parsley.

serving suggestion Flat noodles or a mixture of long-grain and wild rice and a green salad go well with the beef.

tip If you haven't got any Hungarian paprika, which is quite sweet, use 1 teaspoon Dijon mustard instead.

steak au poivre

There is no reason why you can't have an occasional juicy steak on a low-fat plan – lean beef is low in both total fat and saturated fat.

Serves 2 | 295 calories per portion | 11g fat per portion

100ml beef stock
cooking oil spray
2 lean sirloin steaks
(about 200g each)
salt
1 tsp roughly crushed black peppercorns (see Tip)
2 tbsp brandy
2 tbsp half-fat crème fraîche

1 Put the stock in a heavy non-stick frying pan and boil vigorously over a high heat until it has reduced by half – this concentrates the flavours. Pour it into a jug and clean the pan with kitchen paper.

2 Reheat the pan and spray lightly with cooking oil. Sprinkle the steaks with salt and half the peppercorns and cook them on a high heat for 2 minutes each side (for medium rare) or to suit your preference (see Tip).

3 Transfer the steaks to warm plates, add the brandy to the pan and boil for 20 seconds on high. Add the stock, the remaining peppercorns and the crème fraîche, stir and, when the sauce begins to bubble, pour it around the steaks.

serving suggestion Serve the steaks with baked potato wedges or new potatoes, broccoli and mangetout.

tips You could use mixed peppercorns or pink peppercorns, if preferred.
For a rare steak, cook for 1½ minutes each side; for medium cook for 2½ minutes each side; and for well done cook for 3 minutes each side, but it also depends on the thickness of your steaks. A finger test may help – if the steak gives a lot when pressed with a finger, it is rare, and if it is resistant, it is well done.

seared ginger beef and mushrooms

Ginger is a bit like coriander – you either love it or hate it – but in most cases, people who start off hating it, end up loving it!

Serves 2 | 330 calories per portion | 13g fat per portion

1 tbsp groundnut oil

100g broccoli, cut into small florets

300g lean rump steak, cut into strips

3cm piece of fresh ginger, grated or
1 dsp ready-prepared ginger

2 cloves garlic, crushed

125g shiitake mushrooms, sliced
(see Tip)

100g canned bamboo shoots,
drained and sliced

FOR THE SAUCE

1 dsp sauce flour

1 tsp brown sugar

1 tbsp soy sauce

1 tbsp dry sherry

½ tbsp sherry vinegar (see Tip)

1 dsp black bean sauce

50ml beef stock

1 Combine the sauce ingredients thoroughly in a jug or bowl and set aside.

2 Heat the oil in a non-stick wok or large non-stick frying pan and stir-fry the broccoli over a high heat for 2 minutes.

3 Add the beef and stir-fry for 1½ minutes, then add the ginger and garlic and stir to combine.

4 Add the mushrooms and bamboo shoots and stir-fry for 1 minute, then tip in the sauce ingredients, stir well and cook for a further 2 minutes, stirring continuously. Serve immediately (see Tip).

serving suggestion Serve with egg thread noodles.

tips Use oyster mushrooms or chestnut mushrooms instead of the shiitake.

If you don't have any sherry vinegar, substitute white or red wine vinegar instead.

You can garnish the finished dish with fresh basil leaves.

123

quick hob suppers

thai style red curry

Don't be put off trying this great supper by the long list of ingredients – you are likely to have many of them already and they can be converted into a red curry paste in a few seconds using a blender.

Serves 2 │ 320 calories per portion │ 11.5g fat per portion

½ tbsp groundnut oil

1 red pepper, deseeded and thinly sliced (see Tip)

350g lean rump steak, cut into bite-sized cubes

200ml skimmed coconut milk (see Tip, page 34)

FOR THE RED CURRY PASTE

2 fresh red chillies, halved (see Tip)

1 tsp ground coriander seeds

1 tsp ground cumin seeds

2 cloves garlic, peeled

1 stalk (about 6cm) fresh or preserved lemongrass, chopped (see Tip)

1 tsp grated fresh ginger or galangal (see Tip)

2 shallots, halved

1 tsp chilli powder

½ tsp ground turmeric

½ tsp shrimp paste or 1 tsp Thai fish sauce (nam pla)

pinch of salt

1 Put all the red curry paste ingredients into an electric blender and blend to a paste, adding a little drop of water, if necessary.

2 Heat the oil in a non-stick frying pan and sauté the pepper over a medium-high heat for 5 minutes until it is softened, stirring frequently.

3 Increase the heat and add the steak; cook for 1 minute until browned on all sides, then add the red curry paste and stir over a high heat for another 30 seconds.

4 Add the coconut milk and bring to a simmer, then turn the heat down and cook, uncovered, for 20 minutes.

serving suggestion Serve with Thai fragrant rice and a mizuna salad.

tips Instead of the red pepper, you could use 1 large tomato, roughly chopped, in which case add it to the pan after the steak.

Use the chilli seeds unless you want a very mild paste. Jalapeño chillies are milder; bird's eye or Scotch bonnet chillies are hotter.

If you find fresh lemongrass, buy a whole bunch, since the stalks freeze well. You can also buy preserved lemongrass in jars in supermarkets. Don't buy dried lemongrass, which has an inferior flavour.

It is possible to buy grated ginger which has been preserved in small jars, or you could grate your own – a 2cm piece will yield about 1 heaped teaspoon of grated ginger. Galangal is the traditional Thai spice in this recipe, but is not widely available as a fresh root and the dried galangal available in small jars is not so good.

quick hob suppers

steak with garlic and red wine

Serves 2 | 325 calories per portion | 12.5g fat per portion

10g butter

1 large or 2 small shallots
(50g total weight),
very finely chopped

4 cloves garlic, finely chopped

2 lean sirloin steaks
(about 200g each)

salt and black pepper

dash of Worcestershire sauce

50ml red wine

1 tsp Dijon mustard

1 tbsp chopped fresh parsley

1 Heat the butter in a heavy non-stick frying pan and sauté the shallots over a medium-high heat for 3–4 minutes or until softened. Add the garlic and cook for a further 1 minute.

2 Push the shallot and garlic to the sides of the pan, increase the heat to high and add the steaks, sprinkled with some salt and black pepper and a dash of Worcestershire sauce. Cook them for 2 minutes each side for medium rare, or to taste.

3 Transfer the steaks to warm serving plates, leaving behind most of the onion, and add the red wine to the pan with another dash of Worcestershire sauce, the mustard, parsley and a little more seasoning.

4 Stir well, bring to the boil and cook for 30 seconds. Serve the steaks with the sauce drizzled around them.

serving suggestion New potatoes and green beans are ideal with the steaks.

spiced lamb steaks

Serves 2 | 365 calories per portion | 18.5g fat per portion

½ tbsp groundnut oil

2 lamb steaks (about 175g each)

2 shallots, finely chopped

1 clove garlic, finely chopped

½ tsp ground cinnamon

tiny pinch of ground cloves

1 tsp sauce flour

125ml pineapple juice

20ml strong chicken stock

juice of ½ lime

salt and black pepper

1 Heat half the oil in a non-stick frying pan, add the lamb steaks and cook them over a high heat for 2 minutes on each side until browned, then remove with a slotted spoon and set aside.

2 Add the rest of the oil to the pan with the shallots and stir over a medium-high heat for about 6 minutes until softened. Add the garlic and spices and stir for 1 minute (see Tip).

3 Add the flour and stir for a few seconds, then pour in the pineapple juice, stock and lime juice. Season to taste, stir well and bring to the boil.

4 Reduce the heat, return the lamb steaks to the pan and simmer gently for about 10 minutes or until the lamb is cooked and the sauce has thickened. (If the sauce thickens too much, add a little more pineapple juice.)

serving suggestion New potatoes and peas or mangetout are nice with this dish.

tip You could add a finely chopped chilli in step 2 for a slightly hotter flavour.

minted lamb meatballs with pitta

Serves 2 | 440 calories per portion | 17g fat per portion

200g lean lamb, minced
100g spring onion, finely chopped
1 tbsp chopped fresh mint
1 dsp tomato purée
½ tsp ground cumin seeds
salt and black pepper
½ tbsp olive oil
200g cherry tomatoes, quartered
1 tbsp light Greek yogurt
1 tbsp ready-made hummus
juice of ¼–½ lemon
2 pitta breads, to serve (see Tip)
5cm piece of cucumber, roughly chopped, to garnish

1 Mix the lamb with the spring onion, mint, tomato purée, cumin and seasoning and form into 8 small, slightly flattened balls using your hands.

2 Heat the oil in a non-stick frying pan and cook the lamb balls over a medium heat for about 10 minutes, turning once. About two-thirds of the way through the cooking time, add half of the cherry tomatoes and cook until softened, pressing them down a little into the base of the pan.

3 Meanwhile, mix together the Greek yogurt, hummus and lemon juice to taste. Season with salt and pepper.

4 Serve the lamb balls and cooked tomatoes in the pitta breads, filled with the remaining cherry tomatoes and cucumber. Drizzle the hummus dressing over and serve with extra salad.

serving suggestion This is a complete supper but you could add extra salad.

tip Wholewheat pitta breads are slightly lower in calories and higher in fibre than white pittas.

quick hob suppers

pork medallions with sautéd apples

Pork, apples and cider are a typical Normandy combination of flavours, which go really well together.

Serves 2 | 310 calories per portion | 14g fat per portion

½ tbsp groundnut oil

250g pork tenderloin, cut into 1.5cm-thick rounds

1 tsp butter

1 small onion (about 100g), finely chopped

1 red dessert apple, cored and cut into thin wedges

juice of ¼ lemon

1 tsp brown sugar

50ml dry cider

50ml chicken stock

50ml half-fat crème fraîche

1 tsp Dijon mustard

1 dsp chopped fresh tarragon

1 Heat half the oil in a non-stick frying pan and cook the tenderloin over a high heat until browned on both sides (see Tip). Remove the pork from the pan and reserve.

2 Add the rest of the oil and the butter to the pan, reduce the heat a little and sauté the onion for 3–4 minutes, stirring frequently, until softened.

3 Meanwhile, dip the apple wedges in the lemon juice.

4 Add the apple wedges to the pan and sauté for another few minutes until they are slightly golden, then add the sugar and stir for 1 minute.

5 Pour the cider into the pan and bring to the boil, then add the stock and return the meat to the pan. Reduce the heat to low and simmer, uncovered, for 3 minutes or until the pork is cooked all the way through.

6 Stir in the crème fraîche, mustard and tarragon and cook for 30 seconds to warm through, but don't let the sauce boil or the crème fraîche may separate.

serving suggestion Serve with new potatoes and broccoli.

tip If you use a really good quality, heavy non-stick pan, you will need only a smear of oil to brown the pork successfully. Otherwise, give the pan a liberal spray of cooking oil as an additional precaution, which would add about 4 calories and negligible fat per portion.

pork with pak choi and plum sauce

This is very low in calories and fat, but, served with a carbohydrate, such as noodles, makes a substantial meal.

Serves 2 | 255 calories per portion | 8g fat per portion

½ tbsp groundnut oil

225g pork tenderloin, cut into strips

1 tsp grated fresh ginger

1 clove garlic, crushed

4 spring onions, cut diagonally

1 courgette, thinly sliced

150g pak choi, roughly chopped

100g canned water chestnuts, well drained and halved (see Tip)

3–4 tbsp chicken or vegetable stock

1 tbsp soy sauce

2 tbsp plum sauce

1 Heat the oil in a non-stick wok or large non-stick frying pan and stir-fry the next five ingredients over a high heat for 4 minutes.

2 Add the pak choi and water chestnuts – and 1–2 tablespoons of stock if the mixture looks very dry – and stir-fry for another 2 minutes.

3 Add the soy sauce, plum sauce and 1–2 tablespoons of stock, stir well and heat through before serving.

serving suggestion Rice noodles or long-grain rice are simple accompaniments to the pork.

tip If you don't like water chestnuts, or can't find any, use sliced bamboo shoots or mushrooms instead.

129

quick hob suppers

creamy pork with peppers

A warming supper for a winter's evening.

Serves 2 | 320 calories per portion | 12.5g fat per portion

½ tbsp groundnut oil

250g pork fillet (leg or tenderloin),
cut into strips

1 large red pepper, deseeded
and thinly sliced

1 large or 2 small shallots,
finely chopped

1 clove garlic, crushed

1 tsp sweet paprika, plus extra
for sprinkling

1 tsp sauce flour or cornflour

25ml chicken stock

100g small mushrooms, sliced

100ml dry white wine

salt and black pepper

75ml Greek yogurt

1 Heat half the oil in a non-stick frying pan and cook the meat over a high heat until browned on all sides; remove and reserve.

2 Add the pepper and shallots to the pan with the rest of the oil, reduce the heat a little and stir-fry for 4–5 minutes or until softened and just turning golden. Add the garlic and paprika for the last minute of cooking, plus a little water if necessary (see Tip).

3 Add the flour and a dash of the stock and stir for about 20 seconds, then add the mushrooms, wine, the rest of the stock and seasoning, and stir well.

4 Return the meat to the pan and bring to a simmer. Cook gently for 5 minutes, then stir in the yogurt to warm through without boiling. Sprinkle with extra paprika to serve.

serving suggestion Serve with basmati rice or flat noodles and a green salad.

tip When adding water to a stir-fry as a lubricant, add only just enough to moisten the mixture – usually a dessertspoon is sufficient.

bacon, broad bean and potato supper

All age groups seem to like this starchy supper, which is particularly quick to make if you happen to have any leftover cooked new potatoes in the fridge.

Serves 2 | 415 calories per portion | 14g fat per portion

500g new potatoes, halved if large
200g broad beans from a good
quality freezer pack (see Tip)
100g (4 thin rashers) lean back
bacon, cut into strips
cooking oil spray
1½ tbsp olive oil
1 red onion (about 100g), very
thinly sliced
1 tbsp chopped fresh mint
juice of ½ lemon
salt and black pepper

1 Parboil the potatoes in lightly salted water until just about tender; drain and reserve.

2 Meanwhile, blanch the beans in boiling water for 2 minutes; drain and reserve.

3 Cook the bacon strips in a non-stick frying pan, sprayed with cooking oil (see Tip) until golden and slightly crisp, then remove them with a slotted spatula and reserve.

4 Heat the olive oil in the frying pan and sauté the potatoes and onion over a medium-high heat, turning from time to time, until the potatoes are golden.

5 Add the beans, mint, lemon juice and seasoning to the pan, stir, reduce the heat a little and cook for another 1–2 minutes. Stir the bacon into the mixture and serve.

serving suggestion This is a meal in itself but you could add a mixed salad.

tips You could use fresh broad beans but they will need cooking a little longer unless they are very small.

When cooking the bacon, put it in a cold pan and let it heat up to allow the bacon to cook gradually in its own fat. Don't move the bacon until it has sealed on the underside or it may stick to the pan.

spiced chicken with tomatoes

Serves 2 | 295 calories per portion | 12g fat per portion

1 tbsp groundnut oil

1 medium onion, finely chopped

2 cloves garlic, crushed

¼ tsp each ground chilli,
ground cardamom and
ground cinnamon

½ tsp each ground cumin
and ginger (see Tip, page 102)

2 skinless, boneless chicken breasts
(300g total weight), cut into slices

200g fresh tomatoes,
roughly chopped

½ tsp garam masala

salt and black pepper

1 Heat the oil in a lidded, non-stick frying pan and sauté the onion over a medium-high heat for a few minutes until softened, stirring frequently.

2 Add the garlic and spices and stir for another 2 minutes.

3 Add the chicken slices and sauté for 1 minute to colour slightly, then add the tomatoes and all their juice and bring to a simmer. Reduce the heat, cover and simmer gently for 15 minutes.

4 Add the garam masala and seasoning and cook for 1–2 minutes, stirring, uncovered, before serving.

serving suggestion Basmati rice and a green salad are all you need with this dish.

132

stoved lemon chicken

Serves 2 | 295 calories per portion | 15g fat per portion

1 tbsp olive oil

4 skinless, boneless, chicken thighs
(400g total weight – see Tip)

juice of 1 lemon

4 cloves garlic, crushed

1 dsp chopped fresh parsley

1 dsp chopped fresh thyme

50ml dry white wine

25ml chicken stock

salt and black pepper

1 Heat the oil in a lidded, non-stick frying pan and cook the chicken until browned on all sides.

2 Reduce the heat, add the rest of the ingredients and bring to a low simmer, then cover. Cook for 20 minutes or until the thighs are cooked through – when pierced with a sharp knife or skewer the juices run clear.

3 Serve the chicken with any pan juices poured over.

serving suggestion Mashed potato or crusty bread and green beans or broccoli or courgettes are good with the chicken.

tip You can use two chicken breast fillets instead, but the meat may be slightly drier. The cooking time can be reduced by a few minutes if you halve each breast.

chicken fajitas with avocado

Serves 2 | 495 calories per portion | 19.5g fat per portion

300g skinless chicken breast, cut into strips
1 dsp Mexican fajita seasoning (see Tip)
1 tbsp olive oil
1 red onion (about 100g), chopped
1 red pepper, deseeded and chopped
1 yellow pepper, deseeded and chopped
2 tbsp Chilli Salsa (see page 30)
2 ready-made Mexican flour tortillas, to serve

FOR THE SAUCE
½ small ripe avocado, peeled, stoned and flesh chopped
2 tbsp fromage frais, 0% fat
juice of 1 small lime
salt and black pepper

1 Sprinkle the chicken breast strips with the seasoning.

2 Mix together all the sauce ingredients.

3 Heat half the oil in a non-stick frying pan and stir-fry the onion and peppers over a medium-high heat for 5 minutes until softened and turning golden. Remove from the pan with a slotted spoon and reserve in a bowl.

4 Add the rest of the oil and the chicken to the pan and stir-fry for 3–4 minutes until the chicken is cooked through, then return the peppers and onion and any juice in the bottom of the bowl to the pan to heat through.

5 Divide the chicken mixture, salsa and avocado sauce between the tortillas, then roll up and serve in napkins.

serving suggestion These tortillas are a meal in themselves.

tips Omit the chilli from the salsa if you prefer a milder taste.
Fajita seasoning can be found in small packs in the Mexican food section of your supermarket.

133

quick hob suppers

chicken korma

Traditional korma contains a lot of cream and butter but this version keeps the calorie and fat content within bounds.

Serves 2 | 375 calories per portion | 18g fat per portion

½ tbsp groundnut oil

1 medium onion, finely chopped

2 cloves garlic, crushed

1 tsp grated fresh ginger

¼ tsp ground cloves

½ tsp each ground cardamom, cinnamon and chilli

salt and black pepper

½ tsp saffron threads in 1 tbsp hot chicken stock

4 skinless, boneless chicken thighs (400g total weight), each cut into 4

75ml chicken stock

15g shelled cashew nuts (see Tip)

150ml full-fat natural bio yogurt (see Tip)

1 Heat the oil in a non-stick frying pan and sauté the onion over a medium heat for 5 minutes, stirring frequently, until it begins to turn golden. Add the garlic, ginger, dry spices and seasoning and stir for 30 seconds, adding a dash of chicken stock towards the end if necessary.

2 Add the saffron and soaking liquid and the chicken pieces, and stir for 1–2 minutes until the chicken is coloured.

3 Add the chicken stock and bring to the boil. Reduce the heat and simmer, uncovered, for 15 minutes until the chicken is cooked through, by which time much of the liquid will have evaporated.

4 Add the nuts and yogurt and heat through for a few seconds – do not boil.

serving suggestions Basmati rice, mango chutney and a herb salad are perfect curry partners.
A garnish of fresh coriander makes the dish look pretty.

tip For an even creamier taste, you can use full-fat Greek yogurt instead of the natural bio yogurt – if you omit the cashew nuts the calorie and fat count will be almost the same.

green chicken curry

Thai curries have virtually overtaken Indian curries in popularity for home cooking, and although they are a little more trouble, the result is definitely moreish.

Serves 4 | 265 calories per portion | 11.5g fat per portion

½ tbsp groundnut oil

8 skinless, boneless chicken thighs (800g total weight), each cut into 4 pieces

400ml can skimmed coconut milk (see Tip, page 34)

200ml chicken stock

handful of fresh coriander, to garnish

FOR THE GREEN CURRY PASTE (see Tip)

2 shallots or 1 small onion, roughly chopped

2–3 cloves garlic, peeled

2 stalks lemongrass, trimmed and chopped (or use preserved lemongrass in a jar)

4 green chillies, deseeded (see Tip)

2cm piece of fresh ginger, chopped (or use ready-grated ginger in a jar)

1 pack fresh coriander leaves and stalks

juice of 1–2 limes

1 tbsp Thai fish sauce (nam pla)

black pepper

1 Whiz together all the paste ingredients in an electric blender until you have a purée.

2 Heat the oil in a large non-stick frying pan or similar, and stir-fry the paste over a medium-high heat for 1 minute, then add the chicken, coconut milk and stock, then stir.

3 Bring to the boil, then reduce the heat and simmer, uncovered, for 15–20 minutes or until the chicken is tender.

4 Serve garnished with the coriander.

serving suggestion Serve with Thai fragrant rice.

tips It is hardly worth making just two portions of the green curry paste, so if you only want to serve two people, keep the surplus paste in a lidded container in the fridge for a few days, or freeze it.

Only deseed the chillies if you like a milder green curry.

quick hob suppers

chicken and basil sizzle

Basil and coriander are two of the strongest flavoured herbs but they do go well together in this quick Thai-style sizzle.

Serves 2 | 255 calories per portion | 11g fat per portion

2 cloves garlic, peeled
good handful of fresh coriander
(see Tip)
good handful of fresh basil
salt and black pepper
1 tbsp groundnut oil
2 skinless, boneless chicken breasts
(300g total weight), cut into strips
80g baby sweetcorn cobs, halved
2 red chillies, deseeded and
finely sliced
little chicken stock
juice of 1 lime
1 tbsp Thai fish sauce (nam pla)

1 Using a pestle and mortar, pound together the garlic, three-quarters of the fresh herbs and seasoning until you have a coarse paste (see Tip).

2 Heat the oil in a non-stick wok or frying pan and stir-fry the chicken and sweetcorn for 2–3 minutes.

3 Add the chillies and the herb paste and stir-fry for 1 minute, adding a little chicken stock, if necessary, to prevent sticking.

4 Add the lime juice, fish sauce and a little more chicken stock (but you don't want a wet sauce) and stir-fry for 30 seconds until everything is sizzling. Serve garnished with the remaining basil and coriander.

serving suggestion Serve simply with rice or noodles.

tips Don't discard all the coriander stalks for this recipe, since they give a strong coriander flavour and will cook down well as long as you chop them before adding to the recipe.

If you don't have a pestle and mortar, crush the garlic on a chopping board using the flat of a heavy knife, then gradually work in the salt. Finely chop the herbs and mix everything together in a small bowl.

chicken tikka masala

Serves 2 | 310 calories per portion | 13.5g fat per portion

2 skinless, boneless chicken breasts (350g total weight)

½ tbsp groundnut oil

1 clove garlic, crushed

1 tsp each of ground cumin, coriander and turmeric

½ tsp ground chilli

1 tsp grated fresh ginger

1 tsp of sauce flour (see Tip)

salt and black pepper

100ml full-fat Greek yogurt

1 tsp garam masala

1 Slice the chicken breasts into 1cm-thick slices across the grain, then cut these slices into two.

2 Heat the oil in a non-stick frying pan over a medium-high heat and add the chicken, garlic, all the spices (except the garam masala), the flour and seasoning. Stir for a few minutes, adding a spoonful of water, if necessary, to prevent sticking.

3 Reduce the heat, add the yogurt and bring to a very gentle simmer. Cook for 4 minutes, stir in the garam masala and simmer for another 2–3 minutes or until the chicken is cooked through.

serving suggestion Serve with basmati rice, chutney and a green salad, dressed with lemon juice.

tip The sauce flour helps to prevent the yogurt separating, though if it is real Greek yogurt, and you simmer it gently enough, this shouldn't happen.

honeyed duck

Serves 2 | 270 calories per portion | 10g fat per portion

2 skinless Barbary duck breasts (250g total weight), cut into slices (see Tip)

2 tbsp light soy sauce

1 tbsp runny honey

½ tbsp sesame oil

1 red pepper, deseeded and chopped

1 yellow pepper, deseeded and chopped

80g sugar snap peas

6 spring onions, sliced

1 red chilli, deseeded and chopped

1 If you have time, or can plan ahead, marinate the duck slices in the soy sauce and honey while you are at work, or for at least 1 hour.

2 Heat the oil in a non-stick frying pan or wok, and stir-fry the peppers, peas and spring onions for 3 minutes. Add the chilli and cook for another 30 seconds, adding a little water, if necessary, to stop sticking.

3 Add the duck and marinade to the pan and cook, stirring, for 3–4 minutes or until the duck is just cooked.

tip   If you can't find Barbary duck, which has a much better ratio of lean meat to fat than standard duck (Norfolk-type), try to get Gressingham duck, another good meaty variety. This recipe also works well with pork fillet.

turkey and prawn stir-fry

Serves 2 | 355 calories per portion | 12.5g fat per portion

½ tbsp groundnut oil
300g stir-fry turkey meat
6 spring onions, cut diagonally
80g broccoli, cut into small florets
1 tsp grated fresh ginger
1 tsp Chinese five spice
½ tbsp sesame oil
100g oyster mushrooms, roughly torn if large
2 tbsp yellow bean sauce
1 tbsp soy sauce
juice of ½ orange
100g peeled cooked prawns
80g fresh beansprouts
dash of chicken or vegetable stock (optional)

1   Heat the oil in a non-stick wok or frying pan, and stir-fry the turkey, spring onions and broccoli over a high heat for 3 minutes.

2   Add the ginger and five spice and stir-fry for a few seconds.

3   Add the sesame oil and stir in the mushrooms for 30 seconds.

4   Stir in the yellow bean sauce, soy sauce, orange juice and prawns, and cook for another 1 minute.

5   Add the beansprouts and stir-fry for 1 minute, adding a dash of stock if necessary. Serve immediately.

serving suggestions   Serve simply with egg thread noodles.
    Instead of the noodles, you could mix the turkey and prawn stir-fry into Thai fragrant rice or basmati rice. The recipe will then be similar to the Indonesian dish, nasi goreng.

scampi provençal

Serves 2 | 295 calories per portion | 5.5g fat per portion

½ tbsp olive oil

2 medium shallots, finely chopped

3 cloves garlic, crushed

1 jalapeño chilli, deseeded and finely chopped

400g can chopped tomatoes

50ml (about ½ glass) dry white wine

1 bay leaf

black pepper (see Tip)

1 tbsp chopped fresh parsley, plus extra to garnish

400g peeled prawns (see Tip)

1 Heat the oil in a non-stick frying pan and sauté the shallots over a medium heat for a few minutes until softened. Add the garlic and chilli and stir for 1 minute.

2 Add the tomatoes, wine, bay leaf and pepper, stir well and bring to the boil. Reduce the heat and simmer for about 20 minutes or until you have a good sauce.

3 Add the parsley and prawns and simmer for 2–3 minutes to warm through, then serve garnished with a little extra parsley.

serving suggestion Rice and a green salad make simple accompaniments to the prawns.

tips You can use fresh raw prawns: add them to the sauce a little earlier so that they simmer for around 5 minutes and turn pink. The dish will look attractive if the tails are left on the prawns. If using cooked prawns, try to get good quality large ones.

steamed salmon with ginger and chilli

Serves 2 | 330 calories per portion | 19.5g fat per portion

2 tbsp soy sauce

1 tbsp sherry or rice vinegar

juice of 1 lime

2.5cm piece of fresh ginger, grated

2 large spring onions, finely chopped

1 red chilli, deseeded and finely chopped

pinch of caster sugar

2 salmon fillets (about 150g each – see Tip)

½ tbsp sesame oil (see Tip)

fresh coriander, to garnish

1 In a shallow bowl – ideally one which will fit inside your steamer – mix together the first seven ingredients. Add the salmon fillets and turn to coat them in the marinade. If possible, leave to marinate for 30 minutes (but if not, it will still taste fine).

2 Put some water in a large saucepan or in the bottom of a steamer and bring to the boil. Place the bowl containing the fish in the basket of the steamer, making sure there is room around the edges for the steam to rise.

3 Cover the pan and steam the fish for 8–10 minutes or until cooked (but not overcooked).

4 Transfer the fish to warm serving plates. Heat the sesame oil in a small pan. Meanwhile, drizzle a generous amount of the marinade/cooking juices over the fish. Top with the hot sesame oil and garnish with coriander to serve.

serving suggestion Serve with stir-fried mixed vegetables and rice noodles or buckwheat noodles.

tips You can use different fish in this recipe – try bass or bream.
Omitting the sesame oil will reduce the calorie count to 305 per portion and the fat to 16.5g per portion.

tuna catalan

Serves 2 | 335 calories per portion | 17.5g fat per portion

1 tbsp olive oil
1 small onion, finely chopped
1 large red pepper, deseeded and chopped
1 clove garlic, crushed
1 red chilli, deseeded and finely chopped
1 tsp sweet paprika
2 medium ripe tomatoes, roughly chopped
1 dsp sun-dried tomato paste
1 dsp red wine vinegar
salt and black pepper
2 fresh tuna steaks (about 125g each)
1 rounded tbsp ground almonds

1 Heat the oil in a lidded, non-stick frying pan and sauté the onion and pepper over a medium-high heat for 8–10 minutes, stirring from time to time, until softened and just turning golden.

2 Add the garlic, chilli and paprika to the pan and stir for 1 minute, then add the tomatoes, tomato paste, vinegar and seasoning, stir well and cook for another 2 minutes.

3 Reduce the heat, cover and cook for a further 10 minutes or until you have a good sauce (see Tip).

4 Add the tuna to the pan and simmer for 5 minutes, turning the steaks over halfway through. Stir the ground almonds into the dish, check the seasoning and serve.

serving suggestion Green beans and new potatoes are perfect with the tuna.

tip If you like, purée the sauce in an electric blender and dry-fry or grill the tuna separately. Reheat the sauce to serve.

swordfish with chickpeas and spinach

Swordfish is one of my favourite white fish as it is meaty and flavoursome with a dense texture. Unlike some types of fish, it can take strong flavours.

Serves 2 | 315 calories per portion | 11.5g fat per portion

½ tbsp olive oil

1 small onion, finely chopped

2 cloves garlic, well crushed

1 red chilli, deseeded and chopped

400g can peeled plum tomatoes

1 dsp chopped fresh oregano (see Tip)

salt and black pepper

2 swordfish steaks (about 150g each; see Tip)

100g cooked chickpeas (see Tip)

100g fresh baby leaf spinach

1 Heat the oil in a non-stick frying pan and sauté the onion for a few minutes over a medium-high heat, stirring frequently, until softened. Add the garlic and chilli and stir for another minute.

2 Add the tomatoes, oregano and seasoning, stir and bring to the boil. Reduce the heat and simmer very gently for 15 minutes. If the mixture becomes too dry, add a little water.

3 Add the fish steaks and chickpeas to the pan, making sure that the fish makes contact with the base of the pan. Cook for 3 minutes, then turn the fish over and cook for another 2 minutes or until cooked through. Transfer the fish to warm serving plates.

4 Stir the spinach into the sauce and cook for 1–2 minutes until wilted, then serve.

serving suggestion Crusty bread is ideal for mopping up the juices.

tips If you can't get fresh oregano, use basil or mint instead.

Other meaty types of fish that you could use include monkfish, tuna and brill. Pregnant women shouldn't eat swordfish.

Use canned chickpeas, well drained. The remainder can be frozen or you could whiz them up into a vegan sandwich filling with some lemon juice, vegetable stock and seasoning.

quick crabcakes

These hot and spicy little crabcakes are easy to make. Crab is an underused seafood and very low in fat.

Serves 2 | 295 calories per portion | 14.5g fat per portion

200g crab meat

2 spring onions, finely chopped

2 bird's eye chillies, deseeded and finely chopped

3 lime leaves or 1 short stalk lemongrass, finely chopped (see Tip)

1 tsp Thai fish sauce (nam pla)

1 tbsp half-fat mayonnaise

1 handful fresh coriander

dash of Tabasco

30–40g white breadcrumbs

1 tbsp groundnut oil

10g plain white flour

1 lime, cut into wedges, to serve

1 In a bowl, mix together the first eight ingredients thoroughly, then add enough of the breadcrumbs to hold the mixture together so that you can form four small patties.

2 Heat half the oil in a non-stick frying pan. Dredge the patties with flour and fry the cakes on one side for 3 minutes.

3 Add the rest of the oil, turn the cakes over and fry for another 2–3 minutes. Serve with the lime wedges.

serving suggestion Serve with a combination of long-grain and wild rice, a tomato salad or salsa, and Thai dressing used as a dipping sauce (see page 215).

tip Lime leaves are becoming more widely available, but if you don't have them or the lemongrass, use the zest of 1 lime.

ⓥ minted new potato and courgette frittata

An omelette is often a high-fat supper, but this Italian version cuts the fat considerably by including low-fat potatoes and courgettes, reducing the number of eggs needed.

Serves 3–4 | For 3: 325 calories per portion | 16g fat per portion
| For 4: 245 calories per portion | 12g fat per portion

400g new potatoes, cut into bite-sized cubes

2 small to medium courgettes (150g total weight), cut into thin slices

50g baby broad beans (see Tip)

6 medium eggs

salt and black pepper

1 tbsp chopped fresh mint

4 spring onions, chopped

10g butter (about ½ tbsp)

½ tbsp grated Parmesan cheese

1 Cook the potatoes in a saucepan of salted boiling water for 10 minutes or until tender; drain and set aside. Meanwhile, steam the courgettes and broad beans until just tender (see Tip); set aside.

2 Beat the eggs in a large mixing bowl with 1 tablespoon of cold water and season. Add the mint, potatoes, courgettes, broad beans and spring onions, and stir well.

3 Heat the butter over a medium heat in a large non-stick frying pan, swirling it around as it melts so that it doesn't burn. When melted, pour the omelette mixture into the pan and use a fork to spread the vegetables evenly over the base of the pan.

4 Turn the heat down and cook the omelette for several minutes until the base is set and golden (use a spatula to lift a section to see) and the top is beginning to solidify.

5 Preheat the grill to medium. Sprinkle the top of the omelette with Parmesan and brown under the grill for 1 minute, then serve cut into wedges.

serving suggestion Serve simply with a salad.

tips Save using another pan with a collapsible stainless steel steamer, widely available in cookshops. This fits almost any size of saucepan, so you can steam the courgettes and beans over the top of the potatoes as they boil.

You can vary the vegetables used – though I would say the potatoes are essential. Try peas instead of the broad beans and asparagus instead of the courgettes.

ⓥ cheese and potato rosti

If you have a food processor, you can grate the vegetables for the rosti in a few seconds.

Serves 2–3 | For 2: 455 calories per portion | 18g fat per portion
For 3: 305 calories per portion | 12g fat per portion

350g firm-fleshed potatoes (see Tip), peeled and grated

200g orange-fleshed sweet potatoes, peeled and grated

1 Spanish onion, cut into very thin semi-circles and halved again

1 clove garlic, finely chopped

½ tsp ground cumin

1 tbsp chopped fresh parsley

salt and black pepper

1 medium egg, lightly beaten

100g half-fat mozzarella cheese, grated

1½ tbsp olive oil

1 Put both types of potato in a clean teacloth and press well to remove any surplus liquid.

2 Tip the potatoes into a large mixing bowl with the onion, garlic, cumin, parsley and seasoning, and mix well.

3 Add the egg and mozzarella and mix again, then divide the mixture into 2 or 3 (depending on number to serve), or you can cook the rosti whole and cut it up when cooked (see Tip).

4 Heat half the oil in a large non-stick frying pan and add the rosti/s, pressing the mixture down well with a spatula.

5 Cook over a medium heat for 10 minutes or until the base is set and golden (lift an edge with a spatula to check). Add the rest of the oil, turn the rosti/s over and cook for a further 8 minutes or until tender all the way through and golden on both sides.

serving suggestion Serve with a simple salad.

tips You need to use waxy potatoes, not floury ones, otherwise they won't grate well.

Since the rosti mixture is very loose, don't worry if you can't form it into perfect cakes or patties; this doesn't matter, just divide it as best you can if you are serving individual rostis.

ⓥ quick vegetable curry

This curry has a satisfying chunky texture and rounded flavour, so even carnivores won't miss the meat.

Serves 2 | 250 calories per portion | 8.5g fat per portion

100g frozen green beans
150g frozen cauliflower florets
1 tbsp groundnut oil
1 tbsp Dry Spice Mix (see page 221)
6 spring onions, finely chopped
2 large fresh ripe tomatoes, roughly chopped, with their juice
250g butternut squash, peeled and cut into bite-sized cubes
about 100ml skimmed coconut milk (see Tip, page 34)
salt and black pepper
100g fresh baby leaf spinach (see Tip)

1 Defrost the beans and cauliflower in the microwave and pat dry with kitchen paper (see Tip).

2 Heat the oil in a lidded, non-stick frying pan. Add the spice mix and spring onions and cook over a medium-high heat for 1 minute, stirring continuously.

3 Add the rest of the ingredients, except the spinach, (including enough coconut milk to come about three-quarters of the way up the vegetables), and stir well. Bring to the boil, then reduce the heat and simmer, covered, for 15–20 minutes until everything is tender.

4 Add the spinach and simmer for another 2 minutes, uncovered, until wilted, before serving.

serving suggestion Chapati, pitta or basmati rice, low-fat natural bio yogurt and tomato chutney are perfect accompaniments.

tips You can use finely shredded spring greens instead of the spinach.
Using frozen beans and cauliflower saves some time, but if you don't defrost them first, they may make the curry too watery. If you haven't got a microwave, put them in a sieve under running water and dry in a clean tea towel. You can use fresh green beans and cauliflower, but cut the cauliflower small, otherwise it may not cook through in the suggested time.

⊙ falafel patties

People who think they are not going to like these patties are always surprised at how delicious they are – try them!

Serves 2 | 300 calories per portion | 13.5g fat per portion

400g can chickpeas, well drained and rinsed

1 small onion, finely chopped

2 canned red peppers, well drained and finely chopped (see Tip)

1 clove garlic, very finely chopped

1 tbsp chopped fresh parsley

1 tsp ground cumin

1 tsp ground coriander

dash of Tabasco

salt and black pepper

1 tbsp fine polenta or chickpea flour (see Tip)

1 tbsp olive oil

1 Put the chickpeas in a large mixing bowl and mash well with a fork, then add all the rest of the ingredients, except the flour and oil, and combine well.

2 Form the mixture into four or six patties and dredge with the flour.

3 Heat the oil in a non-stick frying pan and cook the patties over a medium heat for 4–5 minutes or until the underside is golden, then turn over and cook for a further 3–4 minutes to brown the other side.

serving suggestion The falafel are delicious stuffed into pitta bread with a green salad and Chilli Salsa (see page 30).

tips Using canned red peppers saves having to roast or grill fresh peppers and skin them. The best canned peppers are called piquillos – they have a great taste.

Using polenta flour gives the patties a nice golden crust – chickpea or gram flour gives a good hue too, but if you don't have either, ordinary plain flour will do.

ⓥ stir-fry ratatouille with mozzarella

Real ratatouille is a stew, cooked long and slow, but this version borrows the Chinese technique to get all that flavour on your plate in less than 30 minutes.

Serves 2 | 230 calories per portion | 12.5g fat per portion

1 tbsp groundnut oil

1 medium red onion, thinly sliced

1 large yellow pepper, deseeded and thinly sliced

2 medium courgettes, thinly sliced lengthways

2 cloves garlic, finely chopped

2 large fresh ripe tomatoes, roughly chopped

salt and black pepper

about 100ml vegetable stock

100g half-fat mozzarella cheese, grated (see Tips)

few fresh basil leaves, to serve

1 Heat half the oil in a wok or large non-stick frying pan and stir-fry the onion and pepper over a high heat for 3 minutes.

2 Add the rest of the oil to the pan with the courgettes and stir-fry for another 3 minutes, then add the garlic and stir for a few more seconds.

3 Tip in the tomatoes, plus all their juice, season well, add half the stock and bring to the boil. Reduce the heat and simmer for 10–15 minutes or until all the vegetables are tender, adding a little more stock if the ratatouille looks dry.

4 Stir in the mozzarella until melted, check the seasoning and stir in the basil to serve.

serving suggestion Crusty French bread is perfect for mopping up the juices.

tips You can use ricotta cheese, which will have a slightly lower calorie count but similar fat content per portion.

Non-vegetarians could, for a change, omit the cheese and stir in 150g chicken fillet, cubed, at the start of the simmering stage. This will have a similar calorie count but nearly 3g of fat less per portion.

149

quick hob suppers

pasta, rice and grains

Pasta and the quick-cook grains, such as couscous, bulgur wheat and instant polenta, form a huge part of any health-conscious cook's repertoire because they are naturally low in fat, cook in minutes, are endlessly adaptable and versatile, marrying well with so many flavours and, of course, are delicious comfort food.

The only problem a fat-watcher may encounter is that pasta, rice and other grains are sometimes served with high-fat, high-calorie sauces or ingredients. Think of cream-laden pasta carbonara, cheese- and meat-heavy lasagne or butter-rich risotto, and you see what I mean!

The twenty-four recipes in this chapter include most of our long-standing favourites, including the above dishes, all 'reworked' to reduce their fat levels to an acceptable minimum; the flavour and texture remain, while the fat and calories are much lower.

There are also plenty of naturally light recipes, such as Linguine with Crab and Coriander, a Sushi Selection and Pasta Primavera. If you're too busy to try even a simple recipe, don't forget that you can create a quick pasta meal using a ready-made tomato sauce, or just a drizzle of olive oil and lemon juice with chopped fresh parsley and basil. You will also find some ideas for using grains in Salads, see page 176.

For successful pasta, you need a large pan and, if serving friends, a large decorative pasta bowl is a good investment. Please note that the cooking times for pasta and grains are only guidelines; since different brands vary, it is best to read the pack instructions first.

pasta carbonara

Many people think of carbonara as one of the richest, most indulgent and high-fat dishes you could choose, but this version brings it well within the parameters of sin-free eating.

Serves 2 | 490 calories per portion | 17g fat per portion

150g dried tagliatelle (see Tip)

10g butter

2 tsp olive oil

2 medium shallots, very finely chopped

3 rashers extra-lean back bacon, cut into thin strips (see Tip)

50ml dry white wine

1 heaped tbsp chopped fresh parsley

50g button mushrooms, thinly sliced

salt and black pepper

1 large egg

2 tbsp half-fat crème fraîche

1 Bring a saucepan of salted water to the boil, add the tagliatelle and cook for 8–10 minutes or according to the pack instructions.

2 Meanwhile, heat the butter and oil in a non-stick frying pan and sauté the shallots over a medium-high heat for 5 minutes, stirring. Push them to the edges of the pan, add the bacon and cook until tinged golden and crispy.

3 Add the wine, two-thirds of the parsley and the mushrooms to the pan with some seasoning. When the wine has started to boil, reduce the heat and simmer for 3 minutes.

4 While the mixture is simmering, beat the egg in a bowl, add the crème fraîche and some seasoning and combine well. By this time the tagliatelle should be cooked, so test, drain and return the pasta to the cooking pan (see Tip).

5 Add the bacon sauce with the egg and crème fraîche mixture to the pasta in the saucepan and heat gently, stirring for a minute until the egg has thickened. Serve in pasta bowls, garnished with the remaining parsley.

serving suggestion Green salad is just the thing to accompany this pasta dish.

tips When cooking pasta, especially when you have other things on the go at the same time, it's a good idea to set a kitchen timer so that you don't forget to tend to it at the end of the cooking time. Pasta quickly overcooks and the amount of time between a perfect 'al dente' and mush may be just a couple of minutes.

Vegetarians can omit the bacon and add an extra 100g mushrooms. The dish would then be about 45 calories less and 4g of fat less per portion.

151

pasta, rice and grains

beef lasagne

Meat lasagne is normally sky-high in calories and fat, but I've reduced both by bulking up the filling with mushrooms and by using sauce flour to make a fat-free béchamel, among other tricks. For a vegetarian version, see Tip.

Serves 4 | 495 calories per portion | 17.5g fat per portion

1 tbsp olive oil

1 large onion (about 200g), finely chopped

1 clove garlic, finely chopped

350g lean minced beef

100g chestnut or portabello mushrooms, finely chopped (include stalks)

400g can chopped tomatoes

1 tbsp tomato purée

dash of Worcestershire sauce

1 tsp fresh oregano

salt and black pepper

about 150ml beef stock

500ml skimmed milk

25g sauce flour

1 tsp Dijon mustard

100g half-fat mature Cheddar cheese, grated

8 no-precook lasagne sheets (see Tip)

2 tbsp grated fresh Parmesan cheese (see Tip, page 72)

1 Heat the oil in a large, non-stick frying pan and sauté the onion over a medium heat, stirring occasionally, for 5 minutes until softened. Add the garlic and beef, and increase the heat a little to brown the meat.

2 Add the mushrooms, tomatoes, tomato purée, Worcestershire sauce, oregano and seasoning, stir well and add the stock. Bring to the boil, then reduce the heat and simmer for 20 minutes or until you have a rich, but still quite liquid, sauce. If the sauce isn't liquid enough, the lasagne won't soften properly and the dish will be too dry.

3 Meanwhile, make a béchamel sauce. Put the milk in a non-stick saucepan with the flour and beat with a whisk over a medium heat until you have a smooth sauce consistency. Cook for another 1–2 minutes, then add the mustard, Cheddar and some salt and stir well for a minute.

4 When the beef mixture is cooked, add a little extra stock or water if it looks too dry and stir well.

5 In a lasagne dish, large enough to serve four, layer half the beef, then half the lasagne, then repeat the layers and pour the white sauce evenly over the top. Sprinkle with the Parmesan and bake in a preheated oven, 190°C/375°F/Gas 5, for 30 minutes or until bubbling and golden.

serving suggestion Serve with a large green salad or a selection of steamed vegetables, such as green beans and courgettes.

tips For a vegetarian lasagne, substitute 300g (cooked weight) brown lentils for the meat (no need to brown in that case) and increase the amount of mushrooms to 150g. The calorie count per portion will be 425 and the fat content 9.5g per portion.

If preferred, precook the lasagne sheets in boiling water for 5 minutes, and use a less liquid sauce: about 75–100ml stock will probably be enough.

spaghetti with meatballs

A true family favourite which makes a nice change from spaghetti à la Bolognese, and it is just as easy to do.

Serves 4 | 525 calories per portion | 13.5g fat per portion

40g white breadcrumbs

40ml skimmed milk

300g lean minced beef or pork

1 tbsp chopped fresh parsley

salt and black pepper

1 medium egg, beaten

1 tbsp olive oil

2 cloves garlic, crushed

400g can chopped tomatoes

1 tbsp sun-dried tomato paste

1 tbsp tomato purée

about 50ml vegetable stock

350g dried spaghetti

1 tbsp fresh basil leaves, torn, to garnish

1 In a mixing bowl, mix together the breadcrumbs and milk, and set aside for 1–2 minutes, then add the beef or pork, parsley and seasoning to the bowl and combine well. Add the egg (or as much as you need to make the mixture bind together), mix thoroughly and form into 20 small meatballs.

2 Heat the oil in a lidded, non-stick frying pan and fry the balls, turning occasionally, over a medium heat until they are browned.

3 Add the rest of the ingredients, except the spaghetti and basil, stir, then bring to the boil. Reduce the heat, cover and simmer for 20–30 minutes or until you have a rich sauce (see Tip). Check the seasoning.

4 Fifteen minutes before the end of the cooking time, bring a large pan of salted water to the boil and when it is bubbling, add the spaghetti, stirring well. Boil for 8–10 minutes, or according to the pack instructions, until the pasta is just tender.

5 Drain the pasta and serve with the meatballs and tomato sauce, with the basil sprinkled over.

serving suggestion Serve simply with a green salad.

tip If the sauce looks too liquid towards the end of the cooking time, remove the lid and cook until reduced. If it looks too dry, add a little more vegetable stock.

pasta, rice and grains

lamb and pinenut pilaf

This is an easy to make, mildly spiced Turkish-style pilaf.

Serves 4 | 530 calories per portion | 19.5g fat per portion

1½ tbsp olive oil

400g lean lamb fillet (leg or neck), trimmed and cut into small cubes

2 red onions, finely chopped

1 yellow pepper, deseeded and finely chopped

225g long-grain rice

½ tsp each of ground cumin, coriander and cinnamon

salt and black pepper

25g sultanas

25g ready-to-eat dried apricots, chopped

½ tbsp each chopped fresh parsley and mint

550ml lamb stock

100ml low-fat natural bio yogurt

good handful of fresh coriander

20g pinenuts, toasted, to serve (see Tip)

1 Heat half the oil in a large, lidded non-stick frying pan and sauté the lamb over a high heat, turning once or twice, until browned. Remove with a slotted spoon and reserve.

2 Add the rest of the oil to the pan with the onions and pepper and sauté over a medium heat for 8 minutes or until softened and turning golden.

3 Add the rice, spices and seasoning, and stir for 1 minute, then return the lamb to the pan.

4 Stir in the dried fruits, parsley and mint, then the stock, and bring to the boil. Reduce the heat, cover and simmer for 30 minutes or until the lamb and rice are tender and the liquid has been absorbed.

5 Stir in the yogurt and coriander and sprinkle the pinenuts on top to serve.

serving suggestion This is a complete meal but you could serve it with some aubergine pickle.

tip Toast the pinenuts in a small, dry non-stick frying pan over a hot heat. Watch them carefully to prevent them burning and turn them over once the undersides have browned.

lamb and orzo gratin

This is a simple baked pasta dish based on a traditional Greek recipe, but it needs to be started in plenty of time as it can't be rushed.

Serves 4 | 465 calories per portion | 15g fat per portion

1 tbsp olive oil
juice of ½ lemon
1 tsp fresh oregano
1 tsp ground cumin seeds
1 tsp ground coriander seeds
salt and black pepper
1 large onion, very roughly chopped into small chunks
450g lean lamb (leg or neck fillet), cut into small bite-sized cubes
550ml passata
200g dried orzo pasta (see Tip)
1 heaped tbsp grated Parmesan

1　In a large mixing bowl, mix together the first five ingredients, season with salt and pepper, then add the onion and lamb and toss thoroughly to combine.

2　Spread the lamb and onion out evenly in a small roasting pan to just fit, and drizzle over the oil mixture left in the bowl.

3　Roast in a preheated oven, 170°C/337°F/Gas 3½, for 45 minutes or until the lamb and onion are lightly golden.

4　Pour the passata evenly over the meat and onion and return the pan to the oven for another 30 minutes.

5　Remove the dish from the oven and stir in the orzo so that it is covered with passata. If there doesn't seem enough liquid in the pan, add some more passata, mixed with a little water, so that the orzo is just immersed.

6　Return to the oven for 30 minutes more, checking towards the end of the cooking time that the pasta hasn't dried out. Taste a mouthful of the pasta to make sure it is tender, then sprinkle over the cheese to serve.

serving suggestion Green beans or a herb salad can be served with the gratin.

tip Orzo is a variety of tiny pasta grains; if you can't find it, use long-grain rice or wholewheat grains, which are available from health food shops.

pasta, rice and grains

salmon with pappardelle and saffron

A delicate yet rich-tasting pasta dish for any occasion.

Serves 2 | 550 calories per portion | 16g fat per portion

150g dried pappardelle
50g petit pois
12 asparagus tips (see Tip)
200g salmon fillet
50ml dry white wine
1 large or 2 small shallots, grated
1 tsp saffron threads in 2 tbsp hot vegetable stock
salt and black pepper
100g fromage frais, 8% fat
fresh dill, to garnish (optional)

1 Bring a large pan of salted water to the boil, add the pappardelle and cook for 10 minutes, or according to the pack instructions.

2 Halfway through the pasta cooking time, put the peas and asparagus on a steamer rack and steam over the pasta for 4 minutes or until just tender.

3 Meanwhile, put the salmon on a plate and microwave on medium-high for 4 minutes or poach gently in simmering water for 4 minutes until just cooked through; flake the fish and reserve.

4 While the pasta, vegetables and salmon are cooking, heat a non-stick frying pan, add the wine, shallots, saffron and stock mixture, and some seasoning and boil for a few minutes until the shallots have softened.

5 Reduce the heat to very low and stir in the fromage frais and combine well. Stir in the peas, asparagus and salmon flakes.

6 When the pasta is cooked, drain and return it to the pan with the contents of the frying pan, toss well to combine and serve garnished with a little dill, if you like.

serving suggestion Serve with a green salad.

tip You can use broad beans or artichoke hearts instead of the asparagus; if you use canned artichoke hearts, they won't need more than a minute's steaming to heat through.

linguine with crab and coriander

Serves 2 | 445 calories per portion | 14.5g fat per portion

150g dried linguine
150g dressed crab meat (see Tip)
1½ tbsp olive oil
juice of 1 lime
1 large jalapeño red chilli, deseeded and finely chopped
good handful of de-stalked fresh coriander
salt and black pepper

1 Bring a large pan of salted water to the boil, add the linguine and cook for 8 minutes, or according to the pack instructions. Drain the pasta and return it to the cooking pan.

2 While the pasta is cooking, combine the crab meat with the remaining ingredients in a bowl.

3 Tip the crab mixture into the drained pasta and toss well to combine before serving.

serving suggestion A green salad is all that is needed to add the finishing touch to this dish.

tip A good mix of white and brown fresh crab meat is best. You could also try good quality frozen crab meat, but avoid the canned version.

fettucine with broad beans and prosciutto

Serves 2 | 460 calories per portion | 13.5g fat per portion

150g dried fettucine (see Tip)
175g shelled weight baby broad beans
cooking oil spray
6 slices prosciutto (Parma ham)
1 tbsp olive oil
juice of ½ lemon
1 dsp chopped fresh mint
1 dsp chopped fresh parsley
salt and black pepper
1 tbsp grated Parmesan cheese, to serve

1 Bring a large pan of salted water to the boil, add the fettucine and cook for 6–8 minutes or according to the pack instructions. Put a steamer rack on top of the pasta and steam the broad beans for about 5 minutes, while the pasta cooks. Remove the beans and set aside.

2 Meanwhile, spray a non-stick frying pan with the cooking oil and add the ham slices. Cook over a medium-high heat until golden, remove from the pan and allow to cool for 1 minute, then crumble roughly in your fingers and return to the frying pan.

3 Add the olive oil, drained beans, lemon juice, herbs and seasoning to the pan and stir over a medium heat for 1–2 minutes.

4 By now the pasta should be cooked, so drain and return it to the pan with the ham and bean mixture, toss well to combine, then ladle into serving dishes and sprinkle with the Parmesan cheese.

serving suggestion Serve with a simple herb salad.

tip Use spaghetti instead of fettucine in this dish, if preferred.

pasta with chicken, ricotta and olives

Serves 2 | 525 calories per portion | 15.5g fat per portion

125g dried farfalle pasta (see Tip)
1 tbsp olive oil
1 medium onion, finely chopped
2 cloves garlic, crushed
2 small skinless chicken breasts (250g total weight), cut into bite-sized cubes
400g can chopped tomatoes
1 tsp fresh thyme leaves
salt and black pepper
8 black stoned olives, halved
50g ricotta cheese (see Tip)
few basil leaves, to garnish

1 Bring a large pan of salted water to the boil, add the pasta and cook for 10 minutes or according to pack instructions, until the pasta is just tender. Do not overcook it, as the shells may break up in the finished dish.

2 Meanwhile, heat the oil in a non-stick frying pan and sauté the onion over a medium-high heat for about 8 minutes until softened and just turning golden. Add the garlic and chicken and cook for another 2–3 minutes until coloured slightly.

3 Tip in the tomatoes, thyme and some seasoning, stir well and bring to the boil. Reduce the heat and simmer for 10 minutes.

4 When the pasta is cooked, drain and add it to the frying pan with the olives and ricotta, then stir gently to combine over the heat for a minute. Garnish with the basil.

serving suggestion Serve with a green salad.

tips Any small pasta shapes are suitable in this dish.
You could use half-fat mozzarella instead of the ricotta, but choose the soft ball kind, not the hard grated type. Cut it into small pieces before stirring it into the sauce, or slice it thinly and place on top of the pasta and chicken, then flash under the grill before serving.

pasta, rice and grains

chicken chow mein

A very quick supper to make because the noodles take only 4 minutes or so to cook.

Serves 2 | 510 calories per portion | 11.5g fat per portion

1 tbsp soy sauce

1 tbsp rice wine or dry sherry

2cm piece of fresh ginger, grated

1 red chilli, deseeded and finely chopped

2 small skinless chicken breasts (200g total weight), cut into thin strips (see Tip)

125g egg thread noodles (two blocks from a standard four-pack)

½ tbsp groundnut oil

1 small red pepper, deseeded and thinly sliced

4 spring onions, thinly sliced on the diagonal

1 medium carrot, cut into julienne strips

50g petit pois

50ml chicken stock

1 tsp sauce flour or cornflour

100g peeled prawns

50g small mushrooms, thinly sliced

½ tbsp sesame oil

1 Mix together the soy sauce, wine or sherry, ginger and chilli in a bowl, and add the chicken. If possible, leave to marinate for 30 minutes or so.

2 Cook the noodles according to the pack instructions, drain and reserve in the pan with a drop of the cooking water.

3 Heat the groundnut oil in a non-stick frying pan or wok and stir-fry the chicken with the pepper, spring onions, carrot and peas for 3 minutes or until the chicken is cooked through and the vegetables are just tender, adding a little stock towards the end of this time, if necessary, to prevent everything from sticking.

4 Add the remaining stock, flour, prawns and mushrooms, and stir for 1 minute.

5 Add the sesame oil and cooked noodles, toss well to combine and warm through for a minute over a reduced heat.

serving suggestion This is a complete meal in itself.

tip You can use strips of pork fillet instead of the chicken.

chicken biryani

This delicious Indian spiced rice dish with fruit, nuts and yogurt is often made with fatty lamb cuts and is very high in fat; this version uses chicken.

Serves 4 | 540 calories per portion | 15.5g fat per portion

1 tbsp groundnut oil
4 skinless chicken breasts, cubed
10g butter
1 large onion, finely chopped
1 clove garlic, crushed
1 tbsp Dry Spice Mix (see page 221)
400ml chicken stock
1 sachet (rounded tsp) saffron threads
225g white basmati rice
50g ready-to-eat dried apricots, chopped
1 tsp garam masala (see Tip)
salt
125ml low-fat natural bio yogurt

TO GARNISH:
25g cashew nuts, toasted (see Tip)
fresh coriander

1 Heat the oil in a large, lidded, non-stick frying pan and sauté the chicken over a high heat, turning once or twice, until golden. Remove with a slotted spoon and reserve.

2 Add the butter and onion to the pan and stir-fry for 5 minutes until softened, then add the garlic and dry spice mix and stir for 1 minute. Meanwhile, heat the stock and add the saffron threads.

3 Add the rice to the spice mixture and stir again, then return the chicken to the pan with the apricots.

4 Pour in the saffron stock, stir and bring to the boil, then reduce the heat, cover and simmer gently for 20 minutes.

5 Stir in the garam masala and a little salt, if needed, and cook for another few minutes. Test the rice – if it isn't cooked and the liquid has been absorbed, add a bit more water or hot stock to the pan and cook for a little longer.

6 Lightly stir in the yogurt and serve the biryani, garnished with the toasted cashew nuts and coriander.

serving suggestion Serve with a tomato and onion salad as well as mango chutney.

tips Garam masala is an Indian spice mix, which is traditionally added towards the end of cooking time to enrich the flavour.
Toast the cashew nuts in a dry non-stick frying pan until golden.

pasta, rice and grains

chicken and seafood paella

Paella looks impressive and makes a good supper party dish.

Serves 4 | 535 calories per portion | 11g fat per portion

1½ tbsp olive oil

2 skinless chicken breasts, each
cut into 4 pieces (see Tip)

1 Spanish onion, chopped

2 red peppers, deseeded
and chopped (see Tip)

800ml chicken stock

1 sachet (rounded tsp)
saffron threads

2 cloves garlic, crushed

275g paella rice (see Tip)

½ tsp Spanish paprika (see Tip)

200g canned peeled plum tomatoes

1 tbsp chopped fresh parsley

100g petit pois

200g mussels in their shells,
cleaned (see Tip, page 23)

200g raw prawns, tails on (see Tip)

salt and black pepper

1 Heat half the oil in a large non-stick frying pan or paella pan and sauté the chicken over a high heat for a few minutes, until browned, then remove with a slotted spoon and reserve.

2 Add the onion and peppers and the rest of the oil to the pan and sauté over a medium-high heat for 8 minutes until softened and turning slightly golden.

3 Meanwhile, bring the stock to the boil with the saffron.

4 Add the garlic, rice and paprika to the frying pan and stir over a medium heat for 1 minute, then tip in the tomatoes and squash them to break them up a little.

5 Add half the parsley and the peas, then pour in the stock and saffron mixture and arrange the chicken evenly in the pan. Bring to a simmer, then reduce the heat and cook the paella gently for 20 minutes without disturbing.

6 Add the mussels and prawns to the paella, pressing them into the rice gently and distributing them evenly, and cook for a further 10 minutes or until the mussel shells have opened and the prawns are pink and cooked through. Season and test the rice to make sure it is tender. (If the paella looks dry before the rice and seafood have cooked, add a little hot water or chicken stock to the pan, but this is unlikely to happen if it is being simmered gently enough.)

7 Serve the paella from the pan, garnished with the remaining parsley.

serving suggestion Serve with a green salad.

tips You can use lean pork fillet instead of the chicken.
   You can use canned piquillo peppers, in which case simply drain and chop them and add to the pan with the garlic and rice.
   You could use any type of long-grain rice if you can't get paella rice.
   If you can't get Spanish paprika, use Hungarian paprika.
   The prawns should ideally be raw, but if using them precooked, get good quality fresh ones, preferably with their tails still on, and add them to the paella for the last 5 minutes of cooking.

mediterranean baked chicken and rice

This is a really moreish dish, which no one will believe is low in fat.

Serves 4 | 505 calories per portion | 10g fat per portion

1½ tbsp olive oil

4 skinless chicken breast fillets, halved

1 large mild onion, thinly sliced

2 red peppers, deseeded and thinly sliced

2 cloves garlic, crushed

1 orange, peeled and segmented

8 black stoned olives, halved

dash of Tabasco

6 sun-dried tomatoes, finely chopped

1 tbsp tomato purée

1 tsp dried herbes de Provence or 1 tbsp mixed chopped fresh herbs (see Tip)

salt and black pepper

225g long-grain rice (see Tip)

400ml chicken stock

1 Heat half the oil in a flameproof casserole (see Tip) and sauté the chicken over a high heat, turning halfway through, for about 3 minutes until browned. Remove with a slotted spoon and reserve.

2 Add the rest of the oil and the onion and peppers, and sauté over a medium-high heat for 5 minutes until softened and turning slightly golden. Add the garlic for the last minute of cooking.

3 Add the orange, olives, Tabasco, sun-dried tomatoes, tomato purée, herbs and seasoning, and stir well, then add the rice and stir again.

4 Pour in the stock, bring to a simmer, then cover and transfer to a preheated oven, 170°C/337°F/Gas 3½, for 45–50 minutes until the chicken and rice are cooked and the stock is nearly completely absorbed. (Check about 10 minutes before the end of cooking time that there is still enough moisture left in the casserole. If not, add a little more hot stock or water.)

serving suggestion A green salad or green beans are good with this dish.

tips You can use parsley, basil, thyme, rosemary and oregano in this dish. If using rosemary, chop it very finely.

You can use brown rice or wholewheat grains, if preferred, in which case add another 20 minutes to the cooking time.

If you don't have a flameproof casserole, cook everything in a large non-stick frying pan up to step 4, then transfer the contents of the pan to a lidded casserole dish.

pasta, rice and grains

sushi selection

Home-made sushi is often much nicer than the ready-made alternative found in supermarkets. It is really quite easy to make and is very low in saturated fat.

Serves 3–4 | For 3: 450 calories per portion | 9.5g fat per portion
| For 4: 335 calories per portion | 7g fat per portion

225g sushi rice
3 tbsp rice vinegar
1 heaped tsp salt
1 tbsp caster sugar
4 sheets nori seaweed
2–3 tsp wasabi paste
75g cucumber, peeled and cut into strips
50g smoked salmon, cut into strips (see Tip)
4 crab sticks or 80g fresh white crab meat
1 small ripe avocado, peeled, stoned and mashed with a little lime juice
80g tuna canned in spring water, drained and lightly mashed
1 canned red pepper, cut into strips (see Tip)
1–2 tbsp soy sauce

1 Rinse the rice in cold water and soak for 1 hour in the cooking pan. Drain and add 450ml fresh water, then bring to the boil. Reduce the heat, cover with a tight-fitting lid, and simmer gently for 15 minutes or until the water has been absorbed.

2 Meanwhile, mix together the vinegar, salt and sugar so that the sugar dissolves. Stir the sugar mixture into the cooked rice and leave to cool.

3 Place a sheet of nori on a sushi mat (see Tip) and spread a quarter of the rice evenly over it, then smear a little of the wasabi paste in a line across the centre (from left to right).

4 Neatly arrange the cucumber and salmon strips along the centre over the paste, then roll up the nori, starting at the end nearest to your body and rolling it away from you. Since the rice is sticky, it will hold together well. Neaten up the ends and cut the roll into 6–8 slices (see Tip).

5 Repeat steps 3 and 4 using the crab and avocado.

6 Repeat steps 3 and 4 using the tuna and red pepper with the two remaining nori sheets.

7 Serve each person a selection of the sushi with the soy sauce for dipping.

serving suggestion You can offer pickled ginger and extra wasabi.

tips Instead of the smoked salmon, use thin strips of raw fresh salmon, marinated in lime juice for 1–2 hours.

You can use fresh red pepper, but you'll need to halve and roast or grill it, then remove the skin before slicing.

If you don't have a bamboo sushi rolling mat, use clingfilm or a napkin.

If you don't want to eat the sushi straightaway, leave the completed rolls wrapped in clingfilm in the fridge and slice them before serving.

jambalaya

This Caribbean dish is hot and spicy and makes a good warm buffet dish.

Serves 4 | 520 calories per portion | 18g fat per portion

1½ tbsp olive oil

1 large Spanish onion, finely chopped

2 medium sticks celery, chopped

1 red pepper, deseeded and chopped

2 cloves garlic, crushed

300g monkfish fillet, cubed (see Tip)

100g chorizo sausage, sliced

225g long-grain rice

1 tsp turmeric

1 tsp chili powder (see Tip)

salt and black pepper

1 tbsp sun-dried tomato paste

1 tsp fresh thyme

500ml chicken stock

175g peeled prawns

25g shelled pistachio nuts

1 Heat the oil in a large, lidded non-stick frying pan and sauté the onion, celery and pepper over a medium heat for 5 minutes until softened, then add the garlic and stir for 1–2 minutes.

2 Add the monkfish, chorizo, rice, turmeric, chili powder, seasoning, tomato paste and thyme, stir well, then pour in the stock and bring to the boil.

3 Reduce the heat, stir, cover and simmer gently for 20 minutes or until the rice is tender. (If the rice isn't cooked and the liquid has been absorbed, add a little more hot stock or water and continue cooking for a few minutes.)

4 Stir in the prawns and nuts and cook for another 1–2 minutes to heat through.

serving suggestion This is a complete meal, but you could serve it with a plain green salad.

tips You can use swordfish instead of the monkfish.

Chili powder (one 'l' not two, as in chilli) is a Mexican-type spice mixture – if you can't find it, use any hot and spicy Caribbean or Mexican mixture.

⊚ three mushroom risotto

This risotto could be served as a starter, in which case it would serve 6–8 people.

Serves 4 | 470 calories per portion | 10g fat per portion

25g dried porcini (cep) mushrooms
100ml boiling water
900ml vegetable stock
15g butter
1 tbsp olive oil
1 medium onion, finely chopped
1 clove garlic, crushed
200g wild mushrooms, cleaned and sliced, if necessary (see Tip)
200g chestnut mushrooms, sliced
350g risotto rice (see Tip)
150ml dry white wine
salt and black pepper
2 tbsp chopped fresh flat-leaf parsley

1 Soak the dried porcini in the boiling water for 20–30 minutes (some take longer than others to soften), then drain, reserving the soaking water, and chop.

2 Add the mushroom soaking water to the vegetable stock to make it up to 1 litre and heat in a saucepan, then keep hot.

3 Melt the butter and oil in a large non-stick frying pan and sauté the onion over a medium-high heat, stirring, for about 8 minutes or until softened. Add the garlic and stir for another minute.

4 Stir in all the mushrooms, dried and fresh, then add the rice and stir for 1 minute. Add the wine and simmer until it has been absorbed.

5 Pour in a quarter of the hot stock and bring to a simmer, stirring frequently.

6 Continue adding a quarter of the stock at a time and stirring frequently until all the stock has been absorbed and the rice is tender – there should still be a bit of moisture left in the pan; the rice shouldn't be dry.

7 Season and stir in the parsley, then serve.

serving suggestion You can serve this with some freshly grated Parmesan cheese – 1 tablespoon adds about 45 calories and just over 3g fat per portion. For a main course, serve a green salad after the risotto.

tips Most supermarkets stock a small range of 'wild' mushrooms, such as chanterelles, morels or fresh porcini (ceps). If you can't get any of those, use large, flat, dark-gilled mushrooms, such as portobellos or field mushrooms.

Use arborio or carnaroli rice for the risotto.

pasta, rice and grains

poached egg and haddock kedgeree

This isn't a traditional kedgeree recipe, as it uses poached eggs rather than hard-boiled, and is cooked in a different way. These changes make it even nicer than the original brunch.

Serves 4 | 530 calories per portion | 16g fat per portion

about 825ml fish or vegetable stock
400g smoked haddock fillet
15g butter
1 tbsp groundnut oil
1 medium onion, finely chopped
1 dsp Dry Spice Mix (see page 221)
300g risotto rice
salt and black pepper
4 medium eggs
1 tbsp chopped fresh parsley
1 tbsp chopped fresh coriander

1 Heat 400ml of the stock in a large frying pan, add the haddock and simmer for 5 minutes or until just cooked, then remove with a slotted spoon, flake into chunks and reserve. Keep the stock in the pan.

2 Add the rest of the stock to the pan and heat to a low simmer.

3 Meanwhile, melt the butter with the oil in a large non-stick frying pan and sauté the onion over a medium-high heat for 8 minutes or until softened and transparent.

4 Stir in the spice mix and cook for 1 minute, then add the rice and seasoning, and stir again.

5 Pour in a quarter of the hot stock and bring to a simmer. When the stock has been absorbed, pour in another quarter, and so on, stirring frequently, until the rice is tender and virtually all of the stock has been absorbed.

6 When you've added the last of the stock to the rice, put some boiling water in the empty frying pan and bring to a low simmer. Break the eggs into the water and poach gently for 4 minutes or until the whites are set and the yolks are still runny (see Tip).

7 While the eggs are cooking, stir the haddock and herbs into the rice to warm through, then serve the kedgeree with an egg on top for each person.

serving suggestion This is a complete meal in itself.

tip If you can't eat partly cooked eggs (if pregnant, for instance), then hard-boil them in their shells, chop and add to the rice with the haddock.

pasta, rice and grains

ⓥ roast vegetable gratin

Although this is a perfect supper dish, it would also make an excellent warm buffet dish and is even good when eaten cold.

Serves 4 | 415 calories per portion | 11.5g fat per portion

1 medium aubergine, cut into
rounds, then halved
2 medium courgettes, cut into
1.5cm thick chunks
2 medium red onions, cut
into 6 wedges
1 fennel bulb, trimmed and cut into
1cm round slices, then halved
2 yellow peppers, quartered,
deseeded, then halved
4 fresh ripe tomatoes, quartered
1½ tbsp olive oil
salt and black pepper
6 cloves garlic, unpeeled
200g dried penne pasta (see Tip)
2 tbsp grated Parmesan cheese
2 tbsp fresh, slightly stale,
breadcrumbs

FOR THE BÉCHAMEL
500ml skimmed milk
25g sauce flour
1 tsp Dijon mustard
1 tbsp capers, well drained
(optional)
1 tsp fresh oregano
100g half-fat mature Cheddar
cheese, grated

1 Put all the vegetables in a large mixing bowl and toss with the oil and plenty of seasoning, then arrange them on a baking tray with the cloves of garlic tucked in well around them. Roast in a preheated oven, 200°C/400°F/Gas 6, for 45 minutes, turning once, or until they are golden and cooked through.

2 Towards the end of the roasting time, bring a large saucepan of salted water to the boil and cook the pasta for 10 minutes, or according to the pack instructions; drain and return to the pan.

3 Meanwhile, make the béchamel sauce. Pour the milk into a non-stick saucepan, add the flour and whisk over a medium heat until you have a smooth sauce. Add plenty of seasoning, stir in the mustard, capers, if using, oregano and Cheddar.

4 When the vegetables are cooked, tip them into a large pre-warmed heatproof serving dish with the drained pasta and the sauce, stirring everything well to combine (see Tip).

5 Preheat the grill to medium. Mix together the Parmesan and breadcrumbs, sprinkle them evenly over the top, and flash under the grill until golden.

serving suggestion This is a complete meal in itself but you could offer a green salad.

tips You can use other pasta shapes, such as macaroni, farfalle, or try flavoured pastas, including tricolour pasta – although I prefer the plain varieties.

Instead of the large heatproof serving bowl, serve the dish in four individual gratin dishes, or you could even bake the cooked pasta and sauce in a roasting pan with the vegetables, sprinkle over the cheese and return it to the oven to brown.

^v pasta primavera

This dish is best served in late spring or early summer when the vegetables are in season and fresh.

Serves 2 | 410 calories per portion | 10.5g fat per portion

150g dried rigatoni
1 tbsp olive oil
2 medium shallots, very finely chopped
1 medium leek, very thinly sliced into rounds
1 medium carrot, sliced lengthways into wafer-thin slices
1 medium courgette, sliced lengthways into wafer-thin slices (see Tip)
50g very young and tender mangetout (see Tip)
1 clove fresh garlic, crushed
2 fresh ripe medium tomatoes, deseeded and roughly chopped
salt and black pepper
2 tbsp half-fat crème fraîche
fresh basil leaves, to garnish

1 Bring a large pan of salted water to the boil, add the pasta and cook for 10 minutes, or according to the pack instructions.

2 Meanwhile, heat the oil in a large non-stick frying pan and sauté the shallots, leek, carrot, courgette, mangetout and garlic over a medium-high heat for 5 minutes, adding a little water if the vegetables dry out.

3 Add the tomatoes to the frying pan with their juices and some seasoning. Stir, bring to a simmer and cook for 4 minutes over a medium-low heat, stirring from time to time.

4 When the pasta is cooked, drain and return it to the pan with the crème fraîche and vegetable mixture. Check the seasoning, toss well to combine and serve garnished with the basil.

serving suggestion This is a complete meal but you can add 1 tablespoon of grated Parmesan cheese to the finished dish, which would add 22 calories and about 1.5g fat per portion.

tips You can use asparagus or broccoli instead of the courgette.
   Petit pois or baby broad beans can be substituted for the mangetout.

171

pasta, rice and grains

ⓥ spaghetti with spinach and ricotta

Serves 2 | 455 calories per portion | 18.5g fat per portion

150g dried spaghetti

2 fresh cloves garlic, peeled

sea salt

1 tbsp good quality olive oil

1 dsp balsamic vinegar

100g baby spinach leaves

75g ricotta cheese

20g pinenuts, toasted

(see Tip, page 154)

1 Bring a large pan of salted water to the boil, add the pasta and cook for 10 minutes, or according to the pack instructions.

2 Meanwhile, pound the garlic with a little sea salt in a pestle and mortar, then add the oil, mix again, and finally the vinegar.

3 When the pasta is cooked, drain, reserving 1 tablespoon or so of the cooking water. Return the pasta and reserved water to the saucepan and over a very low heat, toss it with the garlic and oil mixture. Add the baby spinach leaves and toss for 1–2 minutes until wilted.

4 Stir the ricotta into the pasta mixture to heat through, then ladle into serving bowls and sprinkle the toasted pinenuts over the top.

ⓥ bucatini with lentils and aubergine

Serves 2 | 510 calories per portion | 8.5g fat per portion

80g dried brown or puy lentils

200ml vegetable stock

1 medium onion, finely chopped

400g can chopped tomatoes

1 clove garlic, crushed

salt and black pepper

1 tbsp olive oil

1 medium aubergine, cut into small chunks

150g dried bucatini pasta

1 tbsp chopped fresh parsley, to garnish

1 In a small saucepan, simmer the lentils with the stock and onion for 30–40 minutes, covered, until the lentils are tender. Leave to cool slightly, then purée half the mixture in an electric blender and return it to the pan (see Tip).

2 Add the tomatoes, garlic and seasoning to the pan, bring to a simmer and cook, uncovered, for 5 minutes.

3 Meanwhile, heat the oil in a non-stick frying pan and stir-fry the aubergine over a medium-high heat for 3–4 minutes, adding a little water if it becomes too dry.

4 Add the aubergine to the tomato sauce and simmer for 15 minutes or until everything is tender and the sauce is rich.

5 While the sauce is simmering, cook the pasta in a large pan of boiling salted water until cooked, drain and serve with the sauce, garnished with parsley.

serving suggestion A green salad is all you need with this pasta dish.

tip You needn't blend the lentil mixture, if preferred. It will still be good, but blending gives the sauce a more mature, rich flavour.

ⓥ pasta with garlic mushrooms

Serves 2 | 400 calories per portion | 13.5g fat per portion

150g dried macaroni or farfalle

1 tbsp olive oil

4 spring onions, chopped

100g fresh porcini mushrooms, sliced (see Tip)

4 large cloves garlic, crushed

25ml vegetable stock

salt and black pepper

1 tbsp chopped walnuts

1 tbsp chopped fresh flat-leaf parsley, plus a little extra to garnish

2 tbsp fromage frais, 8% fat (see Tip)

1 Bring a large pan of salted water to the boil, add the pasta and cook for 10 minutes, or according to the pack instructions.

2 Meanwhile, heat the oil in a non-stick frying pan and stir-fry the spring onions over a medium heat for 2 minutes, then add the mushrooms and garlic and stir-fry for another minute.

3 Add the stock and stir for a further minute, then add the seasoning, walnuts and parsley, reduce the heat and stir in the fromage frais. Stir well and heat through – take the pan off the heat if it is still too hot as you don't want the fromage frais to boil.

4 When the pasta is cooked, drain and return it to the pan with the contents of the frying pan. Toss well to combine and serve garnished with some extra parsley.

serving suggestion Serve with a herb salad.

tips If you can't get porcini mushrooms (sometimes called ceps), use chestnut or portobello mushrooms.
    You could use 2 tablespoons of low-fat soft cheese instead of the fromage frais for a similar calorie and fat count.

173

pasta, rice and grains

ⓥ pasta-stuffed peppers

Stuffed vegetables are experiencing a revival in popularity – the usual stuffing is rice or couscous, but this creamy pasta filling makes a nice change.

Serves 4 | 315 calories per portion | 10g fat per portion

125g dried small macaroni or other pasta shapes of choice (see Tip)

2 large red peppers, halved and deseeded

2 large yellow peppers, halved and deseeded

1 tbsp groundnut oil

10g butter

1 large Spanish onion, finely chopped

1 rounded tbsp sauce flour

350ml skimmed milk at room temperature

100g half-fat mozzarella cheese, grated

1 tbsp chopped fresh mixed herbs (see Tip)

1 heaped tbsp finely chopped sun-dried tomatoes (see Tip)

salt and black pepper

cooking oil spray

1 tbsp Parmesan cheese, grated

1 Bring a large pan of salted water to the boil and cook the pasta for 8–10 minutes, or according to the pack instructions, until just tender.

2 Meanwhile, blanch the peppers on a steamer dish on top of the boiling pasta for the last few minutes of cooking. Drain the pasta and reserve, and pat the peppers dry using kitchen paper.

3 Heat the oil and butter in a non-stick frying pan and sauté the onion over a low heat for 15 minutes, until softened and turning golden.

4 Add the flour to the pan, stir well and cook for about 1 minute, then increase the heat a little and gradually add the milk, stirring, until you have a white sauce.

5 Simmer the sauce for 3 minutes, then add the mozzarella, herbs, sun-dried tomatoes and some seasoning, and stir for 30 seconds. Add the drained pasta to the sauce and stir well.

6 Spray a shallow ovenproof dish (large enough to hold the eight pepper halves) with cooking oil and arrange the peppers inside. Spoon the filling into them and top with the Parmesan.

7 Bake for 40 minutes in a preheated oven, 180°C/350°F/Gas 4, or until bubbling and golden. Serve one red pepper half and one yellow pepper half to each person.

serving suggestion Serve with a salad.

tips Use small soup pasta, as the larger the pasta shapes, the less filling you will be able to fit in the peppers.

The ideal mix of herbs is parsley, thyme, mint and oregano, but use what is to hand, although I would avoid coriander and tarragon in this dish.

Choose packets of sun-dried tomatoes, rather than sun-dried tomatoes preserved in oil in jars, as they will be much lower in fat and calories.

ⓥ polenta with tomato and courgette sauce

Polenta is often thought of as very fatty because most recipes suggest adding a great deal of butter and cheese. This version contains just a little but is still full of flavour.

Serves 4 | 295 calories per portion | 10.5g fat per portion

1½ tbsp olive oil
1 litre water
200g quick-cook polenta (see Tip)
1 tbsp mixed fresh herbs (see Tip)
50g fresh Parmesan cheese, grated
salt and black pepper
2 medium to large courgettes, thinly sliced
1 quantity Tomato Sauce (see page 220)
handful of fresh basil

1 Oil a 25 × 15cm baking dish using a third of the oil.

2 Salt the water and bring to the boil in a large non-stick saucepan, then sprinkle in the polenta. Whisking all the time, bring to the boil, then reduce the heat and simmer, stirring frequently, until you have a thick paste that leaves the sides of the pan.

3 Add the herbs and cheese and some seasoning, stir well and quickly pour into the baking dish, smooth down and leave to cool.

4 Brush the courgettes with a third of the olive oil, season well, and griddle or grill for about 3 minutes each side, turning once, until just tender and golden.

5 Meanwhile, heat the tomato sauce in a saucepan or microwave.

6 Cut the cooled polenta into triangles or wedges, brush with the remaining oil and grill or griddle until golden. (If your grill or griddle is large enough, you can do this at the same time as the courgettes.)

7 Stir the basil leaves into the tomato sauce and serve with the polenta and courgettes.

serving suggestion A crisp green salad goes particularly well with the polenta and sauce.

tips Quick-cook polenta grains are readily available in supermarkets. Suitable herbs for this dish include thyme, oregano, rosemary and chives. Use only a small amount of rosemary, though, as it is very strong.

pasta, rice and grains

salads

Salads and slimming would seem to go hand-in-hand – the ultimate cliché for weight watchers is the lettuce and cottage cheese lunch. However, a salad is not necessarily a low-fat feast at all. Many of the most famous salads from around the world, Caesar Salad or Coronation Chicken, for example, are higher in fat than many hot main courses. Additionally, most ready-to-eat salads bought from supermarkets are high-fat, high-calorie little dishes.

Yet you don't have to stick to that lettuce and cottage cheese lunch if you want to eat in a low-fat zone. All the revamped traditional salads in this chapter offer truly healthy, low-fat eating, while still bringing you all the taste, crunch, smoothness, creaminess (or whatever) of the originals.

You'll find reduced-fat versions of the above favourites as well as Italian Roast Pepper and Mozzarella Salad, Greek Salad with Feta, English Egg and Bacon Salad and French Salad Niçoise, plus plenty more tempting ideas – you need no longer suffer at the hands of the limp lettuce leaf.

There are also plenty of fresh and light salads that have become more familiar in recent years: Thai Beef Salad, Chilli Prawn Salad and Thai Pork and Noodle Salad, for example.

The main key to a low-fat salad is a low-fat dressing, but it must not be bland. I've made full use of fruit juices, vinegars, herbs, spices, soy and so on to add plenty of flavour. You'll also find more ideas for basic salad dressings and dips in the Dressings, Sauces and Stocks chapter (page 214).

Many of these salads make ideal starters in half or even quarter portions and all make great lunch or supper dishes.

ⓥ broad bean, mozzarella and sun-dried tomato salad

A clean-tasting salad for a light lunch or supper.

Serves 4 | 175 calories per portion | 11g fat per portion

250g broad beans (see Tip)

salt

40g rocket leaves

50g baby spinach leaves

40g lamb's lettuce

40g sun-dried tomatoes, chopped (see Tip)

1 quantity Reduced-fat Vinaigrette (see page 215)

150g half-fat mozzarella cheese, roughly chopped

1 dsp each of chopped fresh mint and chives, to garnish

1 Cook the beans in boiling salted water for 4 minutes or until tender, then drain.

2 Combine the beans with the salad leaves, sun-dried tomatoes and the dressing, and arrange on four salad plates.

3 Sprinkle the mozzarella over the vegetables and garnish with the fresh herbs to serve.

serving suggestion Olive bread is good with this salad.

tips Use small and tender young broad beans, either fresh or frozen. Otherwise, if you have to use older ones, pop them out of their outer shells and just blanch the tender bright green beans.

Try to use sun-dried tomatoes packed in a vacuum pack or dry-packed in a bag as they contain virtually no fat, whereas those packed in oil in jars are high in both calories and fat.

salads

pasta salad with tomatoes and pesto

This is one of my favourite summer salads, which is good as part of a buffet or you could add some chicken slices to make a more substantial meal.

Serves 4 | 370 calories per portion | 14g fat per portion

250g dried farfalle pasta (see Tip)

salt

2 cloves garlic, crushed

1 tbsp ready-made fresh basil pesto dressing (see Tip)

1 quantity Reduced-fat Vinaigrette (see page 215 and Tip)

200g cherry tomatoes, halved

1 tbsp dry packed, sun-dried tomatoes, finely chopped

12 black stoned olives, halved

bunch of spring onions, chopped

½ bunch of fresh basil

25g pinenuts, toasted, to serve (see Tip, page 154)

1 Cook the pasta in boiling salted water for 8 minutes or until just tender, drain and cool to room temperature.

2 Pound the garlic with the pesto dressing until well combined, then mix thoroughly with the vinaigrette.

3 Toss the pasta, cherry tomatoes, sun-dried tomatoes, olives and spring onions with the dressing. Stir in the basil leaves and sprinkle the pinenuts over to serve.

tips Farfalle are small bow-shaped shapes, but you could also use pasta shells.

Don't buy long-life pesto; get a good quality chilled variety, which you'll find in supermarkets.

Use 1 tablespoon of tomato juice instead of the grape juice in the dressing.

⊙ mushroom and flageolet salad

Serves 4 | 135 calories per portion | 8.9g fat per portion

75g fine French beans, halved

salt

1 quantity Marinated Garlic Mushrooms (see page 28)

½ quantity Reduced-fat Vinaigrette (see page 215)

100g canned piquillo peppers (drained weight), chopped

75g canned flageolet beans (drained weight), rinsed (see Tip)

75g red chard leaves

1 tbsp chopped fresh flat-leaf parsley, to garnish

1 Blanch the French beans in lightly salted boiling water for 2 minutes or until barely tender (or steam for 2 minutes); drain.

2 Remove the mushrooms from the marinade with a slotted spoon and reserve.

3 Mix 2 tablespoons of the marinade with the vinaigrette and toss all the salad ingredients, except the parsley, in the dressing.

4 Serve with the parsley sprinkled on top.

tip You can use borlotti, cannellini or red kidney beans, if preferred.

⊙ bulgur wheat and lentil salad

Serves 4 | 310 calories per portion | 11.5g fat per portion

150g dried puy lentils (see Tip)

1 tsp Dry Spice Mix (see page 221)

150g broccoli florets

about 200ml vegetable stock

75g bulgur wheat (see Tips)

1 red chilli, deseeded and finely chopped

1 dsp fresh thyme

1 quantity Reduced-fat Vinaigrette (see page 215)

8 spring onions, chopped

100g fresh tomatoes, finely chopped

75g feta cheese

1 Cook the lentils in boiling water with the Dry Spice Mix for about 30 minutes, until tender. For the last few minutes of cooking, steam the broccoli over the lentils for 5 minutes or until tender. Drain the lentils and reserve with the broccoli.

2 Meanwhile, bring the vegetable stock to the boil. Pour the hot stock over the bulgur wheat in a heatproof bowl and soak for 20 minutes, or according to the pack instructions.

3 Mix the chilli and thyme with the dressing.

4 Combine the lentils, broccoli, bulgur, spring onions and tomatoes with the dressing. Arrange on serving plates and crumble the feta cheese over the top.

salads

tips You can use ordinary green or brown lentils instead of the puy lentils.
Wholewheat grains can replace the bulgur wheat. Cook as you would brown rice – simmer in lightly salted water for about 30 minutes or until just tender.
You can also use brown rice instead of the bulgur wheat.

roast pepper and mozzarella salad

Serves 4 | 295 calories per portion | 14g fat per portion

2 red peppers, deseeded and each cut into 6 pieces

2 yellow peppers, deseeded and each cut into 6 pieces

1 medium aubergine, cut into 1cm thick rounds

6 good cloves garlic, left whole and unpeeled

1½ tbsp olive oil

salt and black pepper

125g dried penne pasta

1 quantity Reduced-fat Vinaigrette (see page 215)

100g half-fat mozzarella cheese, roughly chopped (see Tip)

1 Toss all the vegetables and garlic in the oil with plenty of seasoning. Arrange on a baking tray and roast in a preheated oven, 200°C/400°F/Gas 6, for 30–40 minutes until golden and tender.

2 Meanwhile, cook the pasta in boiling salted water for 10 minutes or until tender, then drain.

3 When the vegetables are cooked, remove the garlic cloves and press out the soft centres into the dressing. Beat well to combine.

4 Toss the still-warm vegetables with the pasta and dressing, and stir in the cheese before serving.

tip Use the soft, half-fat mozzarella that comes in a ball, packaged in brine; drain and rinse well before using. You can also use halloumi, ricotta or even feta instead of the mozzarella.

181

salads

ⓥ greek salad with feta

Serves 4 | 220 calories per portion | 17g fat per portion

100g cos lettuce, chopped

1 beef tomato, roughly chopped (see Tip)

¼ cucumber, roughly chopped

1 small red onion, very thinly sliced, then separated into rounds

1 yellow pepper, deseeded and roughly chopped

1 quantity Reduced-fat Vinaigrette (see page 215 and Tip)

200g Greek feta cheese

12 black stoned olives (see Tip)

1 handful fresh flat-leaf parsley, to garnish

1 Combine all the vegetables and stir in the dressing.

2 Arrange the salad on four serving plates and crumble over the feta cheese.

3 Top with the olives and garnish with parsley to serve.

serving suggestion Serve with chunks of rustic bread.

tips Pour any juice that escapes when you are cutting the tomato into the salad dressing.

Use 1 tablespoon of lemon juice instead of the grape juice in the dressing.

Try to get Greek Kalamata olives for this salad – they are small and very tasty, and available in jars in most supermarkets.

salads

ⓥ couscous and chickpea salad

Serves 4 | 320 calories per portion | 10g fat per portion

about 200ml vegetable stock

200g couscous

2 tbsp olive oil

2 tbsp lemon juice

1 tbsp ready-made hummus

salt and black pepper

150g canned chickpeas, drained and rinsed

150g fresh tomatoes, chopped

100g cucumber, chopped

1 yellow pepper, deseeded and chopped

1 small red onion, chopped

1 dsp each chopped fresh mint, basil and parsley

1 Bring the stock to the boil and pour it over the couscous in a heatproof bowl. Leave to stand until the stock has been absorbed and the couscous is fluffy and tender.

2 Blend together the oil, lemon juice, hummus and seasoning to make a dressing. If the dressing isn't of a thin pouring consistency, add a little vegetable stock.

3 Tip the couscous into a large bowl, lightly break it up with a fork and stir in the dressing, chickpeas, salad ingredients and herbs.

serving suggestion You can omit the chickpeas and use the salad as a side dish to accompany grilled chicken or a tagine.

ⓥ wild rice, apricot and walnut salad

Serves 4 | 370 calories per portion | 16g fat per portion

200g long-grain and wild rice mix (see Tip)
350ml water, salted
50g ready-to-eat dried apricots, chopped
1 orange, peeled, pith removed, segmented and halved
1 small just ripe banana, chopped
1 stick celery, finely chopped
40g shelled walnut pieces
20g sunflower seeds
1 quantity Reduced-fat Vinaigrette, (see page 215 and Tip)
1 small head white chicory, leaves separated
50g iceberg lettuce, chopped

1 Cook the rice in the salted water in a saucepan, covered, for 20 minutes until the water has been absorbed and the rice is tender (or according to the pack instructions).

2 When the rice has cooled to room temperature, combine all the ingredients, except the salad leaves.

3 Divide the leaves between four serving plates and top with the rice mixture.

tips Brown rice can be used in this recipe instead of the long-grain and wild rice, if preferred. Packs of ready-mixed long-grain and wild rice are available in supermarkets.

Use 1 tablespoon of orange juice instead of the grape juice in the dressing.

183

salads

chicken caesar salad

Caesar salad is normally extremely high in fat but this version retains the spirit of the dish, while being quite light.

Serves 4 | 320 calories per portion | 15g fat per portion

125g ciabatta bread, cut into rough croûtons

300g cos lettuce, leaves torn into pieces

¼ cucumber (about 100g), deseeded and diced

300g smoked chicken breast, cut into slices (see Tip)

4 rinsed and dried anchovies, chopped

25g Parmesan cheese, shaved

FOR THE DRESSING

1 large soft-boiled egg, shelled (see Tip)

2 tbsp low-fat natural bio yogurt

1 tbsp olive oil

1 dsp balsamic vinegar

2 tsp Dijon mustard

1 clove garlic, crushed

dash of Worcestershire sauce

salt and black pepper

1 Bake the croûtons in a preheated oven, 200°C/400°F/Gas 6, for 10 minutes or until they are golden; reserve.

2 Blend all the dressing ingredients together in an electric blender (see Tip).

3 Toss the lettuce, cucumber and chicken with the dressing, and arrange on serving plates.

4 Scatter over the chopped anchovies and the shavings of Parmesan to serve.

tips You can use ordinary cooked chicken, if preferred.

If you don't have a suitable electric blender, simply beat all the dressing ingredients together thoroughly in a mixing bowl using a wooden spoon so that the egg breaks down and combines thoroughly.

This recipe contains partly cooked eggs. If you put the egg into boiling water, it should be ready in about 3 minutes; remove with a slotted spoon and cool under running water for a few minutes to stop it cooking further, then shell it.

coronation chicken salad

This is a good party dish as you can easily make it in large quantities.

Serves 4 | 330 calories per portion | 16.5g fat per portion

500g skinless chicken breasts
400ml chicken stock
1 tbsp groundnut oil
2 shallots, finely chopped
1 rounded tsp Dry Spice Mix
(see page 221)
1 rounded tsp tomato purée
1–2 tbsp mango chutney
mixed salad leaves, to serve
handful of fresh coriander, to garnish

FOR THE DRESSING
100ml half-fat mayonnaise
200ml half-fat Greek yogurt
pinch of sugar
juice of ¼ lemon
salt and black pepper

1 Put the chicken into a saucepan, cover with the stock and poach gently for 15–20 minutes or until cooked through. Remove the chicken from the stock and cut into bite-sized pieces; reserve the stock.

2 Heat the oil in a non-stick frying pan and sauté the shallots over a medium-high heat, stirring frequently, for about 5 minutes or until softened and transparent. Add the spice mix and stir for 1 minute, then add the tomato purée and 50ml of the stock.

3 Put the contents of the frying pan into an electric blender and blend until smooth, then allow to cool.

4 Meanwhile, beat together the dressing ingredients.

5 Pour the shallot blend into the mayonnaise mixture and stir well, then add the mango chutney to taste and combine thoroughly. (Add half the chutney at first as you may find 2 tablespoons is too sweet.)

6 Toss the chicken in the sauce and arrange on a bed of salad leaves, then garnish with coriander.

tip Don't leave the coronation chicken in a warm room for too long and discard any leftovers.

chicken gado gado

*This Indonesian-based salad is a bit more of an effort to put together than some,
but the results are well worth it.*

Serves 4 | 285 calories per portion | 8.5g fat per portion

500g skinless chicken breasts,
cut into 0.5cm strips (see Tips)

4 tbsp soy sauce

225g new potatoes, cut into
bite-sized cubes

salt

100g carrots, cut into julienne strips

100g green beans

100g iceberg, cos or chinese lettuce,
leaves roughly torn

100g cucumber, deseeded and cut
into julienne strips

100g fresh beansprouts

4 large spring onions,
sliced diagonally

handful of fresh coriander, to garnish

FOR THE DRESSING

2 tbsp rice vinegar

juice of ½ lime

1 tbsp caster sugar

1 clove garlic, crushed

1 red chilli, deseeded and
finely chopped

FOR THE GADO GADO SAUCE

2 tbsp smooth peanut butter

4 tbsp skimmed coconut milk
(see Tip, page 34)

1 dsp soy sauce

1 tsp Tabasco

1 tsp runny honey

1 Marinate the chicken in the soy sauce for 20 minutes.

2 While the chicken is marinating, boil the potatoes in lightly salted
water for 15 minutes or until tender. For the last few minutes of the
cooking time, steam the carrots and green beans over the potatoes
on a steaming dish for 3 minutes until they are barely tender; drain
everything.

3 Preheat the grill to medium. Make the dressing by combining all the
ingredients in a small bowl, then make the sauce by beating together
all the ingredients.

4 When the grill is hot, arrange the chicken on the grill rack and cook
for 3 minutes, turning once, or until cooked through.

5 Meanwhile, arrange the lettuce on a serving platter (see Tip) and top
with the potatoes, carrots, beans, cucumber, beansprouts and spring
onions, then drizzle the dressing over the top.

6 Arrange the chicken on top of the salad, spoon the sauce over and
garnish with coriander.

serving suggestion Instead of making one big platter, serve the
salad on four individual dishes.

tips You can cook the chicken on a ridged griddle pan to give it an
attractive striped appearance.

You can use hard-boiled eggs instead of the chicken – use four eggs
and quarter them to serve. This would give 65 calories less per portion but
an extra 2g fat.

thai pork and noodle salad

Serves 4 | 300 calories per portion | 8g fat per portion

1 tbsp groundnut oil

400g pork tenderloin, cut into
0.5cm thick slices (see Tip)

1 dsp fresh grated ginger

150g dried udon noodles

½ quantity Thai Dressing
(see page 215)

50g fresh beansprouts

100g pak choi

handful of fresh basil, to garnish

1 Heat the oil in a non-stick frying pan and stir-fry the pork over a high heat for 2–3 minutes or until browned and cooked through. Add the ginger and stir-fry for 30 seconds.

2 Boil the noodles according to the pack instructions, then drain.

3 Make up the dressing, if necessary, and toss it with the pork, noodles, beansprouts and pak choi.

4 Serve the salad, garnished with basil.

tip You can use chicken fillet instead of the pork for a similar calorie and fat count.

egg and bacon salad

Serves 4 | 210 calories per portion | 15g fat per portion

6 slices lean back bacon
(150g total weight)

4 medium free-range eggs

2 tbsp tomato juice

1 quantity Reduced-fat Vinaigrette
(see page 215)

100g frisée salad leaves

150g ripe tomatoes, quartered

1 red onion, very thinly sliced,
then halved

black pepper

1 Preheat the grill and cook the bacon until crisp, then crumble it with your fingers.

2 Boil the eggs for 5 minutes and cool under cold running water to stop them cooking, then shell carefully (see Tip).

3 Mix the tomato juice into the vinaigrette.

4 Arrange the frisée leaves, tomatoes and onion in four serving dishes and drizzle over the dressing.

5 Sprinkle the bacon over and roughly chop the eggs and arrange on top. Sprinkle them with pepper and serve immediately.

serving suggestion Serve the salad with crusty bread or you could add baked croûtons to the salad – cut 2–3 slices bread into bite-sized pieces and bake in the oven for 10 minutes or until golden.

tip The eggs should not be completely hard-boiled but still with slightly gooey yolks (unsuitable for people who cannot eat partly cooked eggs).

potato and ham salad

Serves 4 | 265 calories per portion | 8.5g fat per portion

800g waxy potatoes, peeled and cut into bite-sized cubes

salt

100g broad beans (frozen are fine; see Tip)

100g prosciutto (Parma ham)

1 small head of white chicory, leaves separated and torn if large, the hearts chopped

½ small head of radicchio, leaves separated and torn if large, the hearts chopped

4 tbsp Reduced-fat Vinaigrette (see page 215)

100g cucumber, deseeded and finely chopped

100g cherry tomatoes, halved

1 dsp each finely chopped fresh mint and flat-leaf parsley

1 Cook the potatoes in boiling salted water for 15 minutes or until tender. Steam the broad beans in a steaming dish placed over the top of them for the last 6 minutes or so of cooking, until they too are just tender, then drain the vegetables.

2 Meanwhile, grill or dry-fry the ham in a non-stick frying pan for 2–3 minutes until it begins to go crisp, then crumble it.

3 Toss the potatoes, bacon, broad beans, chicory and radicchio in the dressing, then stir in the cucumber, cherry tomatoes, mint and parsley to serve.

tip You can use green beans instead of the broad beans.

salads

thai beef salad

A luxurious hot and spicy salad, which is ideal for a winter's lunch.

Serves 4 | 170 calories per portion | 5g fat per portion

cooking oil spray
black pepper
400g fillet of beef in a single joint
½ cucumber (about 200g), halved
lengthways, deseeded and cut
into thin strips (see Tip)
1 romaine or cos lettuce, leaves
roughly torn
50g red mustard leaf or watercress,
thinly sliced
40g hot radishes, very thinly sliced
100g fresh beansprouts
handful of fresh basil, to garnish

FOR THE DRESSING
2 cloves garlic, peeled
4 tbsp Thai Dressing (see page 215)
handful each of fresh coriander
and basil
salt and black pepper

1 Heat a griddle or non-stick frying pan or grill, and spray with cooking oil. Grind some black pepper all over the beef and sear it on all sides until well browned (see Tip). Set aside, cover and leave to cool.

2 Meanwhile, make the dressing. Pound the garlic (preferably using a pestle and mortar) with a little of the dressing, then add the coriander and basil and the rest of the dressing and pound again thoroughly to combine. (As the Thai Dressing is quite salty you may not need any extra salt.) Check seasoning.

3 Thinly slice the beef, which will still be very pink in the middle.

4 Toss the vegetables and beef with the dressing and garnish with basil leaves.

tips Try to get an organic cucumber, which is much tastier and less watery.

When you cook the beef, leave it completely alone for at least 2 minutes so that it seals, otherwise it may stick when you try to move it. Repeat this four times, each time turning the beef by a quarter, so that it browns evenly. Keep the heat as high as you can.

191

salads

tuna salad niçoise

A perennial favourite from the south of France.

Serves 4 | 330 calories per portion | 18g fat per portion

250g Charlotte potatoes (or other new variety), scrubbed and cut into bite-sized chunks, if necessary

salt

75g fine French beans

4 fresh tuna steaks (about 75g each)

3 medium free-range eggs

2 little gem lettuces, outer leaves halved and hearts cut into 6 wedges each

4 vine-ripened tomatoes, quartered

1 red onion, very thinly sliced and separated into rings

1 quantity Reduced-fat Vinaigrette (see page 215 and Tip)

6 anchovies, rinsed, dried and halved

12 black stoned olives, to garnish

1 Cook the potatoes in boiling salted water for 15 minutes or until tender. Steam the beans over the top of the potatoes in a steaming dish for the last 4–5 minutes of cooking, until they are just tender. Drain the vegetables and reserve.

2 Meanwhile, grill, griddle or dry-fry the tuna (see Tip) for 2 minutes each side – a bit less or more, depending on their thickness – then cool for a minute and break into large flakes using your fingers.

3 While the tuna and potatoes are cooking, boil the eggs for about 6 minutes, cool under cold running water, shell and cut into quarters – the centres should still be slightly soft.

4 Arrange the lettuces, potatoes, beans, tomatoes, onion and tuna on serving plates, dividing everything up evenly (or one large platter), and drizzle the dressing over.

5 Top with the egg quarters and anchovies, and garnish with the olives.

tips You can add a clove of crushed garlic and a dessertspoon of finely chopped fresh flat-leaf parsley to the vinaigrette.

If using a frying pan, spray it first with cooking oil (adding 2 calories per portion and negligible fat). If using a griddle, leave the tuna for the complete 2 minutes or so before turning or moving it, otherwise it might stick.

salmon and avocado salad

Most of the fat in this salad is the 'good for you' omega-3 fatty acids or healthy monounsaturated oil.

Serves 4 | 270 calories per portion | 18g fat per portion

350g salmon fillets

16 asparagus tips

1 small head oak leaf lettuce (about 100g)

50g baby red chard or baby spinach leaves

handful of watercress

½ small ripe avocado, peeled, stoned and sliced

8 spring onions, finely chopped, to garnish

FOR THE DRESSING

2 tbsp half-fat crème fraîche (see Tip)

2–3 tbsp skimmed milk

½ small ripe avocado, peeled, stoned and roughly chopped

few sprigs of watercress

1 tsp lemon juice

pinch of caster sugar

salt and black pepper

1 Microwave the salmon on a medium-high heat for 3 minutes, or poach it, until just cooked, then flake (keeping the flakes large, if possible).

2 Steam the asparagus for about 5 minutes until just tender, then refresh under cold running water, pat dry and reserve.

3 Blend all the dressing ingredients together in an electric blender and check the seasoning, adding a little more skimmed milk, if necessary, to make a good pouring sauce.

4 Arrange the lettuce, chard or spinach, watercress, salmon, asparagus and avocado on serving plates and drizzle the dressing over, then garnish with the spring onions.

serving suggestion Brown bread is all you need with this salad.

tip You can use 8% fat fromage frais instead of the crème fraîche, for a slightly creamier, milder tasting dressing. The calorie and fat count will be almost the same.

salads

chilli prawn salad

A simple and quick salad, ideal as a 'pick-me-up' lunch.

Serves 4 | 265 calories per portion | 1.5g fat per portion

200g dried thread (fine) rice noodles

200g small cooked prawns

4 spring onions, thinly
sliced diagonally

1 small green pepper, deseeded and
cut into very small thin strips
(see Tip)

8 large cooked prawns, tails on,
to garnish

FOR THE DRESSING

1 tbsp soy sauce

1 tbsp Thai fish sauce (nam pla)

1 tbsp lime juice

1 tsp caster sugar

1 tbsp skimmed coconut milk

1 dsp chilli dipping sauce

1 tsp ready-grated fresh ginger
(see Tip)

2 red chillies, deseeded and
very thinly sliced

1 Cook the noodles in boiling water, according to the pack instructions – this should only take a few minutes; drain.

2 Mix all the dressing ingredients together.

3 Toss the noodles, small prawns and vegetables in the dressing and divide between four serving bowls. Garnish with the large prawns before serving.

tips You can use a red pepper instead of the green, if preferred. For a less crunchy salad, use a red pepper from a jar or can, well drained; the tastiest ones are piquillo peppers from Spain.

Try to use fresh grated ginger, as the dried ground ginger isn't very aromatic. A reasonable substitute is ready-grated ginger, which is available in small jars in supermarkets.

salads

desserts and bakes

Desserts, puddings and bakes are usually the first meals and treats to go when we are trying to eat less fat and it is true that many are too high in fat to fit comfortably into a healthy eating regime. Yet it is a shame if you do discard them, as they have a lot to offer nutritionally. Many are dairy-based, which is a good source of calcium, often a shortfall in our diets; others are a good source of fibre, vitamins and minerals.

Of course, fresh fruit makes a perfectly satisfactory ending to a meal but now and then everyone needs something a bit different and all fruits can be transformed into the most glorious, tantalising, yet low-fat, puddings and desserts. Bakes also need not be high calorie and unhealthy. My recipes make full use of low-fat dairy produce, wholegrains, fresh and dried fruits, and fat-free ingredients to bring you tasty treats suitable for any occasion. All are suitable for vegetarians, except those using gelatine, in which case agar agar can be used instead.

Even if you don't feel like anything more than basic cooking, there are plenty of quick, healthy ideas for sweet treats that you can try. Grill or bake your fruit instead of eating it raw – bananas grilled in their skins, opened and drizzled with orange juice or low-fat chocolate sauce are lovely, or try strawberries marinated in balsamic vinegar, or baked apples or peaches. Poached dried fruits make a good winter dessert, or you can make a quick summer pudding by poaching summer berries, then soaking pieces of bread in the ruby red juice.

For something quick, creamy and indulgent, try puréed or stewed fruit mixed with low-fat fromage frais and icing sugar, or ready-made meringues crumbled and stirred into Greek yogurt with raspberries. Why? Because you deserve it!

ⓥ raspberry and marsala trifle

An alcohol-enriched trifle is always a treat. This version is also low in fat as an added bonus.

Serves 4 | 235 calories per portion | 5g fat per portion

225g fresh raspberries (see Tip)
3 tbsp water
about 1½ tbsp icing sugar
50ml Marsala wine (see Tip)
1 large banana, thinly sliced
1 dsp raspberry conserve
8 sponge fingers (see Tip)
150g half-fat Greek yogurt
150g fromage frais, 8% fat
150g ready-made low-fat Devon custard

1 Reserve 12 of the best raspberries for decoration and put the rest in a saucepan with the water and 1 tablespoon of the icing sugar, then simmer gently until the juices run free. Add the Marsala and stir. Taste and, if the juice is still sharp, add a little more icing sugar.

2 Add the banana slices to the pan and stir to coat them in the juices, so that they don't turn brown.

3 Spread the conserve on one side of each sponge finger and arrange them in the base of a glass trifle bowl (or in four individual glass bowls, if preferred).

4 Carefully pour the raspberries, juice and banana slices evenly over the top of the sponges and set aside until the juice is absorbed (this will take only a few minutes).

5 Beat together the yogurt, fromage frais and custard with a little icing sugar to taste and spoon the mixture over the trifle/s, smoothing the top.

6 Chill and decorate with the reserved raspberries before serving.

tips Frozen raspberries are perfectly acceptable, if serving this out of season.

Marsala is a fortified Italian wine – if you can't find any, use medium-sweet sherry instead.

You can use three trifle sponges instead of the fingers, in which case, halve them, spread with the conserve, then cut into fingers.

sparkling wine and grape jellies

This is quite a sophisticated jelly, ideal for a light treat to end a dinner party.

Serves 4 | 180 calories per portion | a trace of fat per portion

15g caster sugar

juice of ½ lemon

1 tbsp water

3 tbsp red grape juice, hot

10g powdered gelatine

550ml sweet sparkling
wine (see Tip)

200g seedless red and white
mixed grapes, halved (see Tip)

4 small bunches of whole red
grapes to garnish (about
3–4 grapes each)

1 Dissolve the sugar in a saucepan in the lemon juice and water.

2 Add the hot grape juice to a small heatproof bowl and sprinkle the gelatine over it. Leave for 5 minutes, by which time the gelatine should have dissolved – if not, set it over a pan of just-boiled water until it does.

3 Pour the wine into a large bowl, add the sugar mixture and the gelatine mixture and combine thoroughly.

4 Arrange the grapes in four dessert glasses, then pour equal amounts of the jelly mixture into each. Chill and when half set, stir to distribute the grapes.

5 Continue to chill the jellies until set, and serve garnished with the mini grape bunches draped over the edges of the glasses.

tips Instead of sparkling wine, you could use a dessert wine such as Sauternes, or a non-alcoholic elderflower cordial.
You can use sliced strawberries instead of the grapes, if preferred.

197

desserts and bakes

ⓥ summer berry pavlova

A pavlova isn't difficult to make and meringue is fat-free as well as delicious if the centre is allowed to remain fudgy, which this one is.

Serves 6 | 260 calories per portion | 5.5g fat per portion

4 large free-range egg whites
250g golden caster sugar (see Tip)
1 heaped tsp cornflour
½ tsp vanilla extract
1 tsp white wine vinegar
1 dsp icing sugar
300ml Greek yogurt
350g mixed summer berries, such as strawberries, redcurrants and raspberries (see Tip)

1 Prepare a baking sheet with non-stick parchment.

2 Thoroughly wash and dry a large mixing bowl and an electric whisk, so that there are no traces of grease, oil or damp.

3 Add the egg whites to the bowl and whisk until they form stiff peaks, then whisk in the caster sugar a little at a time until the mixture is thick and glossy.

4 Stir in the cornflour, vanilla extract and vinegar gently to combine. Using a large metal spoon, spoon the meringue on to the centre of the baking sheet, spreading it out a little with the back of the spoon to form a rough round with a slight hollow in the centre.

5 Bake in a preheated oven, 160°C/325°F/Gas 3, for 5 minutes, then reduce the heat to 140°C/275°F/Gas 1, and cook for 1 hour or until golden and firm to the touch. Remove from the oven and allow to cool at warm room temperature.

6 When cool, remove the meringue from the baking parchment. Beat the icing sugar into the yogurt and spread the mixture over the top of the meringue, then top with the fruit to serve.

tips You can use ordinary white caster sugar for a snow-white effect.
   In autumn, use blackberries or autumn crop raspberries for the topping; in spring you could use poached chilled rhubarb. Passion fruit pulp is also a classic topping. You want a slightly 'tart' fruit, rather than anything too bland and sweet, to offset the sugary meringue.

[Ⓥ] ginger plum custard

A warming, easy family pudding for an autumn evening.

Serves 4 | 225 calories per portion | 5g fat per portion

450g red ripe dessert plums, halved and stoned (see Tip)

75g caster sugar

2cm piece of stem ginger, finely chopped

2 large free-range eggs

300ml semi-skimmed milk

½ tsp vanilla extract

1 dsp stem ginger syrup

40ml honey

1 Arrange the plums skin-side up in a shallow ovenproof dish, then sprinkle with a third of the sugar and the stem ginger.

2 Whisk the eggs with the remaining sugar until creamy, then beat in the milk and vanilla, and pour the mixture over the plums.

3 Put the dish in a roasting pan and pour boiling water in the tin to come halfway up the sides of the dish. Bake in a preheated oven, 150°C/300°F/Gas 2, for about 40 minutes or until lightly set.

4 Gently heat the ginger syrup and honey in a small saucepan and drizzle over the plum custard to serve.

tip You can make a similar fruit custard using tinned or fresh poached apricot halves, or baked rhubarb stems, or quartered and peeled ripe dessert pears.

[Ⓥ] strawberry brûlée

A quick and easy version of the classic brûlée, which you will make time and again in the summer.

Serves 4 | 255 calories per portion | 10g fat per portion

250g strawberries, hulled and sliced (see Tip)

1 dsp icing sugar

1 vanilla pod

400ml Greek yogurt

100g caster sugar

1 Arrange the strawberries in the base of four ramekin dishes and sprinkle evenly with the icing sugar.

2 Scrape the seeds from the vanilla pod and stir into the yogurt, then spread the mixture evenly over the fruit in the ramekins and chill for 2 hours.

3 Preheat the grill to high. Sprinkle the caster sugar evenly over the top of the yogurt so that it is well covered.

4 Place the ramekins on a baking tray and flash under the grill – near the heat – for a few minutes until the sugar has melted and is golden and bubbling (see Tip). Remove and serve (the top will set almost straight away).

tips Fresh raspberries, ripe peeled peaches or lightly poached blueberries or blackberries can be substituted for the strawberries. Avoid adding too much liquid with the fruit, as it will spoil the brûlée.

You can use a blow torch to caramelise the sugar – they are obtainable from cookshops or by mail order, starting from around £15.00.

ⓥ summer fruit kebabs

This is the kind of dessert that people who say they can't do desserts will find very easy!

Serves 4 | 135 calories per portion | 4.5g fat per portion

1 dsp runny honey
juice of 1 lime
1 dsp stem ginger syrup (optional – see Tip)
20g butter
dash of rum
150g fresh pineapple chunks
1 large banana, cut into 8 chunks
1 ripe mango, stoned, peeled and cut into bite-sized pieces
1 ripe papaya, deseeded, peeled and cut into bite-sized pieces

1 Put the honey, lime juice, ginger syrup, butter and rum in a small saucepan and warm over a low heat for 1–2 minutes until the butter melts, stirring all the time; set aside.

2 Tip the fruit into the pan with the sauce and stir well to combine, then leave to marinate for 30 minutes, if possible.

3 Preheat the grill to high. Thread the fruits on to four kebab sticks, dividing it evenly.

4 Grill the fruit kebabs, basting with the sauce and turning once, for 5 minutes or until the fruit is golden. Heat any remaining sauce until it bubbles and serve with the kebabs.

serving suggestion You can serve half-fat crème fraîche with the fruit kebabs at 25 calories and 2.5g fat per tablespoon, or full-fat Greek yogurt at 20 calories and 1.5g fat per tablespoon.

tip Jars of stem ginger preserved in syrup are available in supermarkets, but if you don't want to use this, simply increase the amount of honey to 1 tablespoon.

blackcurrant cheesecake

Cheesecake is one of those desserts which fat and calorie watchers always, sadly, try to avoid, so it is marvellous to be able to include this one in your eating plan now and again.

Serves 6 | 245 calories per portion | 12g fat per portion

200g Greek yogurt
150g low-fat soft cheese
150g fromage frais, 8% fat
30g fructose
10g sachet gelatine
3 tbsp hot water

FOR THE BASE
45g low-fat spread
2 tbsp pear and apple spread
(see Tip)
25g wholemeal breadcrumbs
25g rolled oats
25g wholemeal flour
20g ground almonds

FOR THE TOPPING
200g blackcurrants (see Tip)
2 tbsp water
20g fructose
1 rounded tsp arrowroot

1 To make the base, warm the low-fat spread with the pear and apple spread in a mixing bowl for a few seconds in the microwave until runny. Stir together, then add the rest of the ingredients for the base to the bowl and mix thoroughly.

2 Press the base mixture into the bottom of a 20cm non-stick, springform flan tin and bake in a preheated oven, 190°C/375°F/ Gas 5, for 12 minutes, then remove and leave to cool.

3 Meanwhile, make the cheesecake. Mix together the yogurt, soft cheese, fromage frais and the 30g fructose in a mixing bowl.

4 Sprinkle the gelatine over the hot water in a small bowl and leave for 5 minutes, then finish dissolving it over a pan of just-boiled water. Stir 1 tablespoonful of the cheese mixture into the gelatine, then return this to the main cheese mixture and combine thoroughly.

5 Pour the cheesecake mixture on top of the base and chill for 5 hours.

6 For the topping, put the blackcurrants in a saucepan with the water and simmer for 10 minutes or until the juices are running and the blackcurrants are tender. Stir in the 20g fructose until dissolved.

7 Mix the arrowroot with a little cold water, stir into the blackcurrant mixture and simmer for 1 minute until the juice has thickened. Leave to cool, then spoon it over the top of the cheesecake to serve.

tips Several brands of pear and apple spread are widely sold in healthfood shops and delicatessens.

You can make the topping using a can or jar of black cherries – thickening a little of the juice in the same way as above.

ⓥ pears in rosé wine

A pretty way to serve pears in a rich and delicious sauce.

Serves 4 | 220 calories per portion | trace of fat per portion

½ bottle of rosé wine (see Tip)
150ml apple juice
1 sachet mulled wine spices
(see Tip)
75g caster sugar
4 ripe but firm Comice pears,
peeled, leaving the stalks
attached (see Tip)

1 Put the wine and apple juice in a saucepan (see Tip) with the spice sachet and the sugar and warm over a medium heat, stirring, until the sugar dissolves.

2 Put the pears in the saucepan with the stalks uppermost. Add a little water to just about cover the pears.

3 Bring to the boil, then reduce the heat, cover and simmer, for 25 minutes or until the pears are tender – don't overcook them. Remove them from the pan and set aside to cool a little.

4 Return the pan to a high heat and boil, uncovered, for about 15 minutes or until the liquid has reduced to the consistency of a coating sauce (about 200ml).

5 Arrange the pears on a serving dish and pour the sauce over (see Tip).

serving suggestion Serve with a small dollop of half-fat crème fraîche.

tips Red wine is a good alternative to the rosé, although you may need to add a little extra sugar. You can also use all wine instead of part apple juice. Again, you will need an extra 25g sugar or thereabouts.

You can buy sachets of mulled wine spices from wine merchants or from most supermarkets.

Any variety of dessert pear will suffice, although Comice have a superb flavour.

Use a saucepan in which the pears fit tightly, so that they don't fall over. You also will not need too much extra liquid to cover them.

You can leave the pears in the poaching syrup for several hours, basting occasionally, to deepen the pinky red pigment in the pears.

pancakes with pineapple and banana

Pancakes make a good low-fat comfort food for any time of year.

Serves 4 | 245 calories per portion | 5.5g fat per portion

100g plain flour
1 medium free-range egg
300ml skimmed milk
½ tsp salt
cooking oil spray

FOR THE FILLING
15g low-fat spread
200g pineapple pieces in natural juice, drained and juice reserved
2 small bananas, each cut into 12 slices
pinch of ground cinnamon
1 level tbsp soft brown sugar
1 tbsp rum

1   In a mixing bowl, beat together the flour, egg, milk and salt, using an electric whisk if you have one, until you have a smooth, thin batter. You can leave the batter to stand for several hours or it can be used straight away.

2   Spray a good quality, non-stick 18cm frying pan well with cooking oil and heat it over a medium-high heat. When the pan is hot, add about 3 good tablespoons of the batter and swirl it around the pan to cover the base. When the underside is speckled golden (about 1 minute), turn it over using a spatula and cook the other side, then transfer the pancake to a warm plate.

3   Using fresh cooking oil spray each time, cook seven more pancakes this way, then cover and keep them warm (see Tip).

4   Melt the low-fat spread in the frying pan over a medium-high heat and add the pineapple, bananas and cinnamon. Cook for several minutes, stirring occasionally, until the bananas begin to colour.

5   Add the sugar and stir well to dissolve, then add the rum and stir again for 1 minute. Add 2–3 tablespoons of the pineapple juice to make a little sauce and heat through.

6   Divide the mixture between the pancakes, then fold them into quarters to serve.

tip If the pancakes are cold, warm them in the microwave on medium-low for a minute.

desserts and bakes

ⓥ strawberry and nut gâteau

By using a fatless sponge and a creamy low-fat filling, you have a special treat for dessert or afternoon tea.

Serves 6 | 225 calories per portion | 9g fat per portion

7g butter

3 medium free-range eggs

100g caster sugar

75g plain flour, plus extra for dredging

FOR THE FILLING

275g low-fat soft cheese

100g low-fat fromage frais

2 tbsp icing sugar, plus extra for dusting (optional)

1 dsp lemon juice

250g small ripe strawberries, hulled

1 tbsp strawberry coulis

25g chopped mixed nuts

1 Use the butter to grease 2 × 18cm sandwich tins, then line with greaseproof paper and dredge with flour.

2 Put the eggs and sugar into a large heatproof (such as Pyrex) mixing bowl, placed over a pan of very hot water and whisk, using an electric whisk, until the mixture is pale and light and leaves a trail when the whisk is removed.

3 Remove the bowl from the heat and whisk until cool. Sift half the flour into the mixture and fold it in lightly with a spatula. Repeat with the rest of the flour.

4 Pour the mixture evenly into the tins and bake in the centre of a preheated oven, 190°C/375°F/Gas 5, for 20 minutes or until risen and the centre springs back when pressed gently with a finger. Turn out from the tin, remove the greaseproof paper and leave to cool on a rack.

5 Meanwhile, make the filling (see Tip). Mix the soft cheese with the fromage frais and beat in the icing sugar and lemon juice, then halve the mixture.

6 Cut half of the strawberries into two and set aside. Chop the other half of strawberries fairly small and mix these with half of the soft cheese filling.

7 When the sponges are cool, skewer them in several places and drizzle the strawberry coulis over so that it seeps into the cake. Spread half of the strawberry and cheese mixture over one of the sponge halves, then lay the other sponge on top.

8 Spread the remaining cheese mixture on top and sprinkle the nuts over, then lightly press the remaining strawberries, cut-side down, into the topping. Dust with a little icing sugar to serve.

tip Instead of the cheese and strawberry filling, you can make a citrus one by boiling the juice of 1 orange and 1 lemon with 2 tablespoons maple syrup and 1 tablespoon Grand Marnier in a saucepan. Skewer the basic sponge and drizzle the citrus liquid over.

ⓥ bread and butter pudding

This is an interesting take on the traditional layered bread and butter pudding with only a tenth of the fat.

Serves 4 | 230 calories per portion | 5g fat per portion

50g sultanas

50g ready-to-eat dried apricots, chopped

150ml apple juice

20g butter

1 tsp mixed spice

125g slightly stale bread, cut into small cubes (see Tip)

1 large banana, chopped

150ml skimmed milk

1 tbsp golden caster sugar

1 Put the dried fruits, apple juice, butter and spice in a saucepan and stir over a medium heat until the butter has melted.

2 Add the bread and banana to the pan and stir well.

3 Tip the mixture into a shallow ovenproof dish and spread it out evenly. Pour the milk over everything and sprinkle with the sugar.

4 Bake in a preheated oven, 190°C/375°F/Gas 5, for 30 minutes until golden brown.

serving suggestion Half-fat custard or Greek yogurt are delicious with this pudding.

tip Brown or white bread is fine but it should be good quality. You could also use brioche, which would add just a few calories and 1g of fat per portion.

desserts and bakes

chocolate mousse with raspberry coulis

An easy dessert for chocolate lovers – you will need four pudding moulds about 150ml capacity.

Serves 4 | 190 calories per portion | 6g fat per portion

2 tbsp cocoa powder

350ml skimmed milk

2 medium free-range eggs, separated

70g caster sugar

1 tsp vanilla extract

3 tbsp hot water

12g gelatine

25g plain chocolate shavings or chocolate flakes, to decorate

FOR THE COULIS

150g fresh or frozen raspberries

1 dsp lemon juice

20g icing sugar

1 Mix together the cocoa powder and milk in a saucepan and heat to boiling point, then leave to cool for 5 minutes.

2 Meanwhile, beat the egg yolks with the sugar, using an electric whisk, until thickened and creamy, then stir in the vanilla.

3 Gradually pour the milk mixture into the egg mixture, stirring all the time to combine.

4 Return the mixture to the pan and stir over a very low heat for 5 minutes until thickened a little.

5 Put the hot water in a bowl, sprinkle the gelatine over and leave for a few minutes to dissolve; place the bowl over a saucepan of hot water, if necessary. Stir it into the milk mixture thoroughly and leave to cool until it begins to set.

6 Whisk the egg whites until they form soft peaks and fold them into the milk mixture. Divide the chocolate mousse between four moulds and leave to set in the fridge.

7 To make the coulis, purée the raspberries (defrosted, if necessary) with the lemon juice in a blender, then put through a sieve to remove the pips and stir in the icing sugar.

8 To serve, unmould the mousses by running them under hot water for 1 minute, then arrange them on plates with the chocolate shavings or flakes sprinkled over and the coulis poured around.

desserts and bakes

ⓥ christmas cake

This cake is best made near to Christmas, though it will keep in an airtight tin for a week or two. It is less 'crumbly' than a standard Christmas cake but does taste delicious.

Makes 16 × 100g slices │ 320 calories per portion │ 8.5g fat per portion

600g mixed dried fruit
75g cut mixed peel
100g glacé cherries, halved
3 tbsp brandy
200ml apple juice
100g stoned ready-to-eat prunes
100ml water
100ml runny honey
100ml sunflower oil
grated zest of 1 orange and 1 lemon
300g plain flour
2 rounded tsp baking powder
2 rounded tsp mixed spice
50g ground almonds
3 egg whites

1 The day before you want to make the cake, put the dried fruits in a large mixing bowl. Stir the brandy into the apple juice and add this to the fruits, stirring well. Cover and leave overnight.

2 Cook the prunes in the water in a small saucepan, covered, for about 15 minutes or until softened. Cool and blend in an electric blender (liquid included) to make a purée the consistency of a thick sauce.

3 Warm the honey (this will take a few seconds in a microwave) and put it in the blender with the oil and prune purée, blend for a few seconds and pour it over the fruit mixture. Add the fruit zests and mix well.

4 Sieve the flour and baking powder into a bowl and stir in the spice and almonds, then incorporate the flour into the fruit mixture in three or four batches, stirring.

5 Whisk the egg whites in a clean and dry bowl until light and fluffy, then fold them into the fruit mixture until well combined. Lift a spoonful of the mixture up to see if it falls off the spoon easily; if not, add a little more apple juice until it does.

6 Grease and line a 20cm round baking tin with baking parchment and spoon the mixture in, pressing down well and smoothing it out. Cover with a layer of baking parchment (see Tip) and bake in the centre of a preheated oven, 150°C/300°F/Gas 2, for 1¾ hours or until a skewer inserted into the centre comes out clean.

7 Leave to cool in the tin for 30 minutes, then turn out, remove the parchment and cool on a rack (see Tip).

tips Tie a thick layer of brown paper around the outside of the cake tin to prevent the outside from burning before the centre is cooked. You can also sit the tin on a sheet of cardboard.

You can decorate the cake with a selection of crystallised fruit slices.

Skewer the cake once or twice and pour a little brandy into the holes in the few days after the cake is made to enrich the flavour.

chocolate chip muffins

A taste of chocolate is always a nice treat when you're watching your fat intake.

Makes 12 | 190 calories per portion | 4g fat per portion

300g plain flour
2 tsp baking powder
150g golden caster sugar
50g chocolate chips, milk or plain (see Tips)
1 large free-range egg
225ml skimmed milk
2 tbsp sunflower oil
1 tsp vanilla extract

1 Arrange 12 muffin cases in a 12-cup muffin tin.

2 Sift the flour and baking powder into a mixing bowl and stir in the sugar and chocolate chips.

3 In another bowl, combine the egg, milk, oil and vanilla, beating well.

4 Tip the milk mixture into a well in the flour mixture and mix together quickly – don't overmix or the muffins will become tough; you don't need a smooth mixture.

5 Spoon the mixture into the muffin cases and bake in a preheated oven, 200°C/400°F/Gas 6, for 15 minutes or until the muffins have risen and are golden and firm in the middle when lightly pressed with a finger. Cool on a rack and serve warm or cold (see Tip).

tips You can buy ready-prepared chocolate chips in small bags at the baking counter in supermarkets. For a little extra luxury, buy 50g good quality Belgian chocolate and chip it yourself – refrigerate or freeze it until very hard, put inside a plastic bag and crack with a rolling pin until you have small pieces.

You can use 100g fresh blueberries instead of the chocolate, which will save 16 calories and 1g fat per portion.

These muffins will keep for a day.

desserts and bakes

ⓥ apricot and apple flapjacks

Flapjacks make a good lunchbox addition and are always a welcome treat.

Makes 9 squares | 215 calories per portion | 9g fat per portion
12 oblongs | 160 calories per portion | 7g fat per portion

50g golden syrup
125g half-fat butter or margarine
50g soft brown sugar
juice of ½ lemon
pinch of salt
60g ready-to-eat dried apricots, finely chopped
20g sunflower seeds
225g rolled oats
1 dessert apple, peeled, cored and grated
25ml apple juice

1 Warm the syrup, butter or margarine and sugar in a small saucepan, and stir over a low heat until the butter has melted and the sugar has dissolved.

2 Add the lemon juice, salt, apricots and seeds, and stir well.

3 Remove from the heat and add the oats, stir gently to combine but don't overbeat.

4 Stir the apple and juice into the oat mixture, then press the mixture into a shallow baking tin, about 20cm square.

5 Bake in a preheated oven, 190°C/375°F/Gas 5, for 20 minutes or until golden. Mark into squares or oblongs while still warm, so the flapjacks are easy to cut when cold.

ⓥ banana bread

This is a moist teabread, which is as satisfying as a slice of cake but much lower in fat.

Makes 8 slices | 160 calories per portion | 4.5g fat per portion

100g self-raising flour
75g wholemeal self-raising flour
1 tsp baking powder
40g butter
50g soft dark brown sugar
1 level tsp mixed spice
60ml skimmed milk
2 ripe bananas, mashed

1 Grease and line a 450g (1lb) loaf tin with baking parchment (see Tip).

2 Sift the flours and baking powder into a mixing bowl, then rub in the butter until the mixture resembles fine breadcrumbs.

3 Stir in the sugar and spice, then stir in the milk and bananas, and mix well.

4 Spoon the mixture into the loaf tin and bake in a preheated oven, 180°C/350°F/Gas 4, for 40 minutes or until the loaf has risen and is golden and firm in the centre, and when a skewer inserted into the centre comes out clean.

5 Turn out and cool on a wire rack.

serving suggestion You can spread slices of banana bread with a little low-fat spread at 20 calories and 2g fat per teaspoon.

tip You can double the quantity of the mixture and cook in a 900g (2lb) loaf tin, or make double quantity in 2 × 450g (1lb) tins and freeze the second one.

⊚ sultana malt loaf

A malt loaf is one of the lowest-fat bakes you can make and it is moist and delicious.

Makes 8 slices | 175 calories per portion | 2g fat per portion

125g strong plain flour
100g wholemeal flour
½ tsp salt
1 tsp easy-blend yeast
1 tbsp soft brown sugar
125g sultanas
2 tbsp malt extract
½ tbsp black treacle
1 tbsp sunflower oil
100ml skimmed milk
flour, for kneading

FOR THE GLAZE
2 tsp caster sugar
1 tbsp boiling water

1 Grease and line a 450g (1lb) loaf tin with baking parchment.

2 Sift the flours and salt into a mixing bowl. Add the yeast, then stir in the sugar and sultanas.

3 Warm the malt extract, treacle and oil in a small saucepan until runny but not too hot, and add this to the mixing bowl, then stir in the milk.

4 Mix to a soft sticky dough and turn on to a floured work surface.

5 Knead for 10 minutes or until the dough is elastic and smooth, then shape it roughly to fit the tin. Put the dough in the tin and leave, covered, in a warm place to rise for 1–2 hours.

6 Bake in a preheated oven, 200°C/400°F/Gas 6, for 30 minutes until golden and the base sounds hollow when tapped.

7 Dissolve the caster sugar in the boiling water and brush the top of the loaf to glaze while it is still in the tin, straight out of the oven. Leave to stand for 10 minutes, then turn the loaf out and cool on a rack.

desserts and bakes

dressings, sauces and stocks

Many hundreds of grams of fat and very many calories can be consumed in the form of salad dressings, dips, sauces for meats and fish, and so on. Yet I am not a great believer in making strange and complicated low-fat concoctions for salads – and similar – that aim to replace the high-fat versions, but which always seem to turn out a disappointment in both flavour and texture.

In general, the best idea is to choose sauces and dressings that are naturally low in fat, such as salsas, Thai-style dips and dressings, vegetable-based sauces, and spice mixtures, or creamy yogurt-based sauces like tzatziki or raita.

The selection of 'extras' in this chapter are all included because they are delicious in their own right, whether you are fat and calorie watching, or not. Even the Reduced-fat Vinaigrette and the Mayonnaise substitute, while not being quite as unctuous and wonderful as their full-fat versions, are nevertheless perfectly satisfactory, and both will save you masses of calories if you eat a lot of salad or are a compulsive mayonnaise-dipper.

I have also given basic recipes for stocks, as a good stock is easy to prepare and can make the difference between an excellent sauce, stew or soup and an indifferent one. Otherwise, use good quality ready-made chilled stock, or, in the case of vegetable stock, use Marigold bouillon, which is very acceptable and comes in a low-salt version.

If you don't want to make your own, Heidelberg make an acceptable range of low-fat dressings. There are many other low-fat brands on the market but few are really delicious.

ⓥ reduced-fat vinaigrette

Makes enough to dress a salad for 4 people │ 60 calories per portion │ 6g fat per portion

2 tbsp extra-virgin olive oil
1 tbsp balsamic vinegar
1 tbsp red grape juice (see Tip)
1 tsp Dijon mustard (see Tip)
1 tsp caster sugar
salt and black pepper

1 Put all the ingredients in a screw-top jar and shake vigorously to combine.

2 Taste and adjust the seasoning as necessary (see Tip).

serving suggestion Use in the appropriate recipes in this book or for any salad that requires French dressing or vinaigrette.

tips You can use white grape juice, if preferred.
You can use either wholegrain Dijon mustard or the smooth type.
The dressing will keep for 1–2 weeks in the fridge.

thai dressing

Makes 8 tablespoons │ 10.5 calories per portion │ negligible fat per tablespoon

2 tbsp rice vinegar
2 tbsp lime juice
1½ tbsp Thai fish sauce (nam pla)
1 tbsp caster sugar
1 clove garlic, crushed
1 hot red chilli, deseeded and very finely chopped (see Tip)

1 Put all the ingredients in a screw-top jar and shake vigorously to combine.

2 Leave for several hours, shaking once or twice, so that the sugar has thoroughly dissolved and the flavours have time to mingle.

serving suggestion This is good on any Thai-style meat or fish salad and you can also use it on a plain salad to serve with grilled or roast meat or crabcakes (see page 143).

tip If you want a really hot dressing, you can leave the chilli seeds in.

dressings, sauces and stocks

ⓥ low-fat mayonnaise

Makes 4 tablespoons | 28.5 calories per portion | 2.5g fat per tablespoon

2 tbsp low-fat natural
bio yogurt (see Tip)
1 tbsp reduced-fat, ready-
made mayonnaise
1 dsp lemon juice (see Tip)
1 tsp smooth Dijon mustard
salt and black pepper

1 Beat together the yogurt and mayonnaise in a mixing bowl, using a wooden spoon.

2 Stir in the lemon juice, mustard and seasoning and stir again; check the seasoning.

3 Chill before serving (see Tip).

tips I always use bio yogurt because it has a mild and creamy flavour with no hint of sourness.

You can use lime juice instead of the lemon juice, and add 1 teaspoon of Thai fish sauce (nam pla) for a slightly spicy sauce to go with grilled prawns or salmon.

This will keep for 1–2 days, covered, in the fridge.

sauce verde

Makes 10 tablespoons | 28 calories per portion | 2.5g fat per tablespoon

50g anchovies, rinsed and dried
(see Tips)
50g capers, rinsed and dried
(see Tips)
15g fresh flat-leaf parsley
15g fresh basil
1 clove garlic, crushed
1 tbsp extra-virgin olive oil
1 tbsp red wine vinegar (see Tip)
1 tsp smooth Dijon mustard
black pepper

1 Roughly blend the anchovies, capers, herbs and garlic in an electric blender and transfer to a mixing bowl.

2 Add the remaining ingredients and stir very thoroughly to combine. Check the seasoning – you are unlikely to need any salt as the anchovies are salty.

serving suggestion This piquant sauce is great with plain grilled fish and is good as a marinade too.

tips Small cans of anchovies can be found in most supermarkets. The capers are usually kept near the olives and pickles.

You can omit the anchovies and capers for a milder sauce, or add white wine vinegar instead for a greener sauce.

ⓥ tartare sauce

Makes 4 servings | 30 calories per portion | 2g fat per portion

1 tbsp half-fat mayonnaise

2 tbsp full-fat Greek yogurt

1 shallot, very finely chopped

25g capers, rinsed and dried

25g gherkin, rinsed, dried and finely chopped

salt and black pepper

1 In a serving bowl, combine the mayonnaise and yogurt and stir in the shallot.

2 Add the capers to the bowl with the gherkin and some black pepper. Stir everything well and taste – add a little salt if you think it necessary.

3 Leave for a few hours in the fridge, if possible, for the flavours to mingle and stir again before serving. (The sauce can be lightly warmed in the microwave for a few seconds.)

serving suggestion The sauce is an excellent accompaniment to white fish and makes a good dip for crisps or crudités.

ⓥ coriander coconut relish

Makes 4–6 servings | For 4: 65 calories per portion | 4.5g fat per portion
For 6: 45 calories per portion | 3g fat per portion

juice of 1 small (or ½ large) lime

1 pot fresh coriander

2 cloves garlic, crushed

2 green jalapeño chillies, deseeded and chopped

100ml low-fat natural bio yogurt

25g desiccated coconut

salt

1 Put the lime juice, coriander, garlic and chillies into an electric blender and whiz until you have a coarse paste.

2 Put the yogurt and desiccated coconut in a serving bowl and season with a little salt.

3 Stir in the coriander paste and chill for a few hours to allow the flavours to develop, if possible.

serving suggestion This goes well with most Thai curries and other spicy savoury dishes. It is also good as a dressing for a chicken sandwich, instead of the more fattening tikka masala dressing, and can be used as a dip with tortilla chips.

dressings, sauces and stocks

ⓥ mango and pineapple salsa

Makes 4–6 servings | For 4: 50 calories per portion | 0.5g fat per portion
For 6: 35 calories per portion | trace of fat per portion

1 ripe mango, stoned, peeled and
cut into 1cm chunks,
juice reserved
200g can crushed pineapple pieces
in juice, drained and juice
reserved
1 tbsp balsamic vinegar
zest of ½ lemon or lime
1 dsp finely chopped fresh mint
1 green jalapeño chilli, deseeded
and very finely chopped (see Tip)
salt and black pepper

1 Put the mango and any juice in a bowl.

2 Add the pineapple and 1 tablespoon of the juice to the bowl.

3 Add the remaining ingredients to the bowl and stir well to combine, taste to check the seasoning, cover, and chill for 1 hour to allow the flavours to mingle.

serving suggestion This salsa goes well with chicken, turkey and barbecued dishes.

tip You can omit the chilli, if you prefer.

sweet and sour dipping sauce

Makes 6 tablespoons | 25 calories per portion | negligible fat per tablespoon

3 tbsp rice vinegar
2 tbsp caster sugar
1–2 tbsp soy sauce

FLAVOURINGS
lime juice to taste
1–2 very finely chopped red chillies
1–2 cloves garlic, crushed
piece of fresh ginger, finely grated
1–2 teaspoons of Thai fish sauce
(nam pla) or more to taste

1 Put the vinegar and sugar in a small non-stick saucepan and heat gently until the sugar has dissolved. Increase the heat until the mixture is bubbling and cook for several minutes until you have a thickish syrup.

2 Stir in the soy sauce and a little water, if necessary. Taste and adjust the amount of soy, if necessary. Add flavourings from the choices given.

serving suggestion Use as a dip for Thai dumplings, prawns, satay sticks, fishcakes, sushi or crudités.

dressings, sauces and stocks

218

ⓥ tomato and onion salsa

Makes 4–6 servings │ For 4: 85 calories per portion │ 6.5g fat per portion
For 6: 55 calories per portion │ 4.5g fat per portion

2 large ripe tomatoes, deseeded
and finely chopped

6cm piece of cucumber, deseeded
and finely chopped

1 red pepper, deseeded and
cut into 1cm squares

1 small red onion, finely chopped

1 handful of fresh coriander (see Tip)

2 red jalapeño chillies, deseeded
and finely chopped

1 quantity Reduced-fat Vinaigrette
(see page 215 and Tip)

salt and black pepper

1 Put the tomatoes and cucumber into a mixing bowl.

2 Add the remaining ingredients to the bowl and combine thoroughly
(see Tip). Taste to check the seasoning, adding a little more salt and
pepper, if necessary. Chill the salsa until needed.

serving suggestion This goes well with fishcakes, grilled fish or
meat, burgers and barbecues.

tips You can replace the coriander with fresh flat-leaf parsley. If you are a
great fan of coriander, don't discard the stalks but chop them very finely
and add to the salsa for a stronger flavour.

Use 1 tablespoon of lime juice instead of the grape juice in the dressing.

You can add 100g drained, canned beans to the salsa – borlotti or red
kidney beans are ideal. This would add about 25 calories and a trace of fat
per portion (for 4).

ⓥ tomato sauce

Makes 4 servings | 65 calories per portion | 3g fat per portion

1 tbsp olive oil
1 medium onion, finely chopped
1 clove garlic, crushed
400g can chopped tomatoes
1 dsp tomato purée
1 tsp soft brown sugar
juice of ½ lemon
salt and black pepper

1 Heat the oil in a non-stick frying pan and sauté the onion over a medium-high heat, stirring from time to time, until softened and transparent.

2 Add the garlic and stir for 1 minute.

3 Add the remaining ingredients, stir well and bring to the boil (see Tips). Reduce the heat and simmer, uncovered, for 30 minutes or until the sauce has thickened and is rich.

serving suggestion This is good as a pasta sauce or in any recipe where a rich tomato sauce is called for. It can also be used as a 'side' sauce for grilled fish, chicken, turkey or vegetable burgers.

tips Add 2 mild Jalapeño-type chopped chillies and use wine vinegar instead of the lemon juice for a slightly spicy sauce.
Add chopped fresh parsley towards the end of the cooking time, or add chopped basil just before serving.
Add a pinch of ground ginger and cumin for a warming sauce.
Add extra garlic and some chopped black olives for a tasty pasta sauce.

ⓥ harissa paste

Makes 4 tablespoons | 65 calories per portion | 6.5g fat per tablespoon

2 tbsp olive oil
4 red jalapeño chillies, deseeded and chopped
4 cloves garlic, roughly chopped
1 tbsp ground cumin seeds
1 tbsp ground coriander seeds
1 tsp salt
Tabasco, to taste

1 Put all the ingredients in an electric blender and blend until you have a paste.

2 Use as directed in the recipes using harissa in this book or transfer to a lidded container and store in the fridge – it will keep for a week or more.

serving suggestion Use the chilli paste in Moroccan recipes such as Grilled King Prawns with Harissa (see page 62), or Middle Eastern Vegetable Soup (see page 42), to add heat and flavour to soups, stews and casseroles, or as a marinade for fish and meat.

laksa paste

Makes 4 servings | Made using oil: 70 calories per portion | 7g fat per portion
Made using water: 15 calories per portion | 1g fat per portion

1 stalk lemongrass, outer leaves removed and centre finely chopped
2 red chillies, deseeded and halved
1 tsp ground galangal (see Tip)
1 dsp grated fresh ginger
1 shallot, roughly chopped
small handful fresh coriander
2 tbsp groundnut oil (see Tip)
1 tsp shrimp paste
½ tsp turmeric
½ tsp ground paprika
1 tbsp tamarind paste
½ tsp caster sugar

1 Put all the ingredients in an electric blender and blend to a paste, adding a little water, if necessary.

2 If not using immediately, transfer to a lidded container and store in the fridge, where it will keep for a week or so.

serving suggestion The paste forms part of the traditional Malaysian laksa recipe (see page 34). It can also be used as a spice blend for fish, meat and chicken curries.

tips Galangal is a ginger-like root often used in far eastern cooking.
You can omit the oil and use extra water instead, although the paste will not be quite as good.

dry spice mix

Makes about 7 tablespoons | 10 calories per portion | trace of fat per tablespoon

3 tbsp ground turmeric
2 tbsp ground coriander seeds
1 dsp ground cumin seeds
1 tsp each of ground cardamom seeds, chilli, cloves, ginger and black pepper

Combine all the spices together in a mixing bowl. Transfer to a lidded container and store in a cool, dark, dry place (see Tips). Use as directed in the recipes in this book, e.g. Poached Egg and Haddock Kedgeree (see page 169), Quick Vegetable Curry (see page 147) or Coronation Chicken Salad (see page 185), or in your own curries, soups and casseroles.

tips It is best to buy spices whole and grind them yourself, particularly coriander, cumin and black pepper. Ground spices quickly lose their flavour.
A good way to grind spices is in a coffee grinder, kept especially for the purpose. A pestle and mortar will crush spices but not as thoroughly as a grinder.
The spice mix will keep for a few weeks before losing its flavour and aroma.

dressings, sauces and stocks

^v basic vegetable stock

Makes 1 litre | negligible calories

1 onion, chopped
2 carrots, chopped
1 leek, chopped
2 sticks celery, chopped
1 bouquet garni
several black peppercorns
salt
1 litre water

1 Put all the ingredients in a lidded saucepan and bring to the boil.

2 Skim off any foam that forms on the top, reduce the heat and simmer for 30 minutes.

3 Allow to cool a little, strain through a sieve and cool. Discard the vegetables and use the stock within 24 hours or freeze.

chicken stock

about 60 calories | 5g fat for the whole quantity

Add a whole uncooked chicken carcass to the recipe above and cook for 2 hours, then cool and strain. When cold, skim any fat off the surface and use as directed in the recipe.

fish stock

about 30 calories | 1g fat for the whole quantity

Follow the basic vegetable stock recipe but omit the carrots and leek and add 1kg raw fish bones and trimmings to the water. Simmer for 30 minutes, strain and cool.

meat stock

about 60 calories | 5g fat for the whole quantity

Follow the basic vegetable stock recipe but add 500g raw red meat bones and lean trimmings to the water. Cook for 3 hours, strain and cool, then skim any fat off the surface.

tips Roast the bones and meat trimmings in a preheated oven, 180°C/350°F/Gas 4, for 1 hour before adding to the water for extra flavour.
   Once the stock is strained, cooled and skimmed of fat, as necessary, you can increase its flavour. Tip the stock into a saucepan and boil rapidly until reduced – the more you reduce it, the stronger it will become.

index